T0171473

The Joy of Work

*How to Stay
Calm, Confident & Connected
In a Chaotic World*

Dr. Stephen G. Payne

BALBOA.
PRESS

A DIVISION OF HAY HOUSE

Copyright © 2013 by A New Equilibrium. All rights reserved.
www.ANewEquilibrium.org

Artwork and graphics by Dr. Stephen G. Payne.

This book is a work of non-fiction. Names of people and places
have been changed to protect their privacy.

No part of this book may be used or reproduced by any means, graphic, electronic,
or mechanical, including photocopying, recording, taping or by any information
storage retrieval system without the written permission of the publisher except
in the case of brief quotations embodied in critical articles and reviews.

Balboa Press books may be ordered through booksellers or by contacting:

Balboa Press
A Division of Hay House
1663 Liberty Drive
Bloomington, IN 47403
www.balboapress.com
1-(877) 407-4847

Because of the dynamic nature of the Internet, any web addresses or links contained in
this book may have changed since publication and may no longer be valid. The views
expressed in this work are solely those of the author and do not necessarily reflect the
views of the publisher, and the publisher hereby disclaims any responsibility for them.

The author of this book does not dispense medical advice or prescribe the use of any
technique as a form of treatment for physical, emotional, or medical problems without the
advice of a physician, either directly or indirectly. The intent of the author is only to offer
information of a general nature to help you in your quest for emotional and spiritual well-
being. In the event you use any of the information in this book for yourself, which is your
constitutional right, the author and the publisher assume no responsibility for your actions.

Any people depicted in stock imagery provided by Thinkstock are models,
and such images are being used for illustrative purposes only.
Certain stock imagery © Thinkstock.

Printed in the United States of America

ISBN: 978-1-4525-6585-9 (sc)
ISBN: 978-1-4525-6586-6 (e)

Balboa Press rev. date: 01/30/2013

Acknowledgements

A New Equilibrium, the organization driving the ideas behind this book, is far more than good ideas about joyful working and living. It is also a community of committed professionals who believe in the ideas, practice them and support each other in the community.

Thank you, from the bottom of my heart, to all the people in the community who have helped me with this book. I am especially grateful to the Trustees and Advisors of A New Equilibrium, my coaching clients and those leaders who willingly shared their thoughts and critiques of manuscripts.

My deepest thanks for the specific practical contributions and support from Terry Adams, Allison Ashley, Joyce Avedisian, John Baker, Amanda Banfield, Raymond Bonwell, Nancy Bugbee, Robert Campbell, Sharon D'Agostino, Brother Daniel, Bill Deeter, Drew Deeter, Gerry Dehkes, Don Deieso, Joseph Durko, Phil Herman, Terry Herring, Alan Horgan, Kevin Hrusovsky, Liz Hughes, Sabine Hutchison, Bart Jackson, Paul Kayne, Dan Kibbe, Terri Ledva, Martyn Lee, Lorraine Marchand, Peter Marchesini, Howard Matalon, Kevin McDermott, Michael McNamara, Jeanne Murphy, Keith Newton, David Panzarella, Ryan Parsons, Mark Roskey, Mary Ann Ryan, Anne Sawbridge, Tim Stewart, Bob Weinhold, Meghan Weiss, Maria Wetzel, Jim Wood, Ryan Yu, Lou Zoppel, and Jan Marie Zwiren.

Special thanks to Linda Cooper, ANE's Administrative Officer, my fine editors, Simon Jarvis and William Payne, my publishing manager and copy editor, Nora Bass, my designer, Lisa Marien, and all the team at Balboa.

And, above all, to Amy for a lifetime of supporting my dreams.

Introduction: The Inner Core

There's this place at the soul of our being. It's where the essence of everything that's good about us exists and wants to have greater influence in the world.

Do you know yours? Do you care for yours?

You might call it your sense of purpose, your destiny, God, your courage, or even your inner drive. I picture mine as my inner core. It's deep, it's inspiring, and it has tremendous power to improve my life.

When I pause and really focus on my inner core, intentionally caring about all the good I possess that's trying to come out into the world, I get a strong feeling of certainty. Any sense of lacking starts leaving me. I feel more whole and complete, exactly where I need to be, ready to expand. I'm filled with a deep sense of joy.

Whatever situation I'm in, at work or at home, I always get the best result when I consciously make this inner core connection.

Yes, there are feelings of doubt and difficulty in my inner core, too. They distract me, blur my focus, and limit my power. But I'm constantly learning ways to stay connected to the good at my inner core rather than yielding to the frustration of the negative.

People around me, especially those I lead, feel it, too. They often say it inspires them. What I see and love is our powerful connection, and the way incredibly productive conversations have taken my entire life journey down pathways I never dreamed possible.

I used to be always searching to get more. More, more, more. I needed to know I was making a difference, that my life mattered. What I actually got from wanting more and more was feeling less and less satisfied. I felt let down so often. Do you know that feeling of "more of the same" is not working, but you are less and less able to put your finger on a better way?

Studying books, changing my environment, and practicing new leadership tools worked for short periods, but they didn't stick. I kept investing time, money, and energy to be more successful and ending up unfulfilled at a deeper level.

Things changed quickly when I decided to expand my connection to my inner core. More control over my circumstances and myself followed. My confidence in a better future grew. Lasting results came, not by grasping, but as a natural consequence of my inner growth. I got the deeper kind of joy I was always really seeking.

It's not really that complicated. By managing my sense of equilibrium at my inner core, I'm able to consciously release more of my own inner passion and joyful spirit into situations. The whole process opens permanent pathways to success I never imagined possible.

The purpose of this book is to help you feel greater joy in your work life and beyond by opening yourself to the pathways uniquely available within you. This is not a manual; it's more an invitation to a journey that reveals and strengthens the unique connection between you and your inner core to enhance your sense of meaning, confidence and connection to others. By sharing my journey, and those of business leaders who have kindly volunteered theirs, we hope that the ideas and tools will spark an improved and more joyful pathway for you.

How would it feel to enjoy more of your true significance, to know for certain that your life's work is worth it? Would people respond to you better or worse?

What would it be like for you to feel a constant sense of confidence, a sense of clarity and complete certainty, that not only do you have command of your situation, but also you are exactly where you need to be? Would you enjoy seeing that confidence rub off on those around you?

And what about your sense of satisfaction, your sense of belonging, your sense of fun, your sense of your time being valuable, your sense of your power, your sense of your integrity…?

Could expanding your connection with your inner core reveal a better and more joyful pathway for you?

Welcome to the caring community of leaders and professionals we call A New Equilibrium. Let's start the journey.

Dr. Stephen G Payne
Princeton, New Jersey

Table of Contents

There are three parts, each with chapters laced with practical ideas and experiences of people who are joyfully succeeding by learning to connect themselves and others to their inner core. At the end of each part, there are five "Moments of Reflection" for you to consider for your life and career.

Part 1 describes the story behind the inner core, how business leaders successfully develop their spiritual core and the resulting joy and calm they experience when they are fully tuned into their powerful center.

Part 2 offers concepts, tools and examples to help shape your inner core connection. Greater confidence is the result. Through real stories of business leaders, connect to your own unique pathway to more joy.

Part 3 shows you the substantial, positive shift in your connection to people from this book's approach. Learn how to use this book's core concepts to inspire and motivate others—your friends, colleagues, and teams—even lifting the joy of an entire major corporation.

Part 1: Calm

Discovering A New Equilibrium

"Leaders become immobilized by the pace of change. It takes being sharpened to a whole deeper reality to restore the wonderfully joyful feeling that all the senses are back working again."
— Kevin Hrusovsky, CEO, Caliper Life Sciences

"I have let people and objects and activities come toward me and impinge on me till I have been over-piled and mountain-covered with thoughts. But now I know that I AM at my own Center..."
— Emma Curtis Hopkins, *The Radiant I AM*

Chapter 1

The Core of Leadership

A Satisfying Work Life

I have such a passion for talking with business leaders. I love to dig into the depths of how and why they lead. Over many hundreds of meetings, I've come to realize that those who achieve the greatest satisfaction and joy in life have this incredible connection to the truth of who they really are. There's a deep inner trust, peace, and certainty they exude wherever they go.

In today's chaotic business world, who wouldn't want more of that?

Do you get enough joy and certainty from your work? Not just the outward fame and fortune bits, but also the inner part of how you feel at a deeper level. How happy are you that your life and job are on an upward trajectory?

Here's a simple test.

Do your conversations with friends and colleagues ever include saying you are constantly "stretched far too thin," or your work and family are "totally out of balance," or you're suffering "the agony of job changes," or you're working for "a boss who is such a [insert your usual expletive]?" These phrases are symptoms of a deeper yearning not being satisfied.

What happens to us is this: The high pressure to perform, generated by others and ourselves, without a strong connection to our own inner core (that is our calm, confident and connected inner self), causes a loss of inner balance. We become unnecessarily anxious and adrift. That's when we start using these complaining phrases with people. Our sensitive inner core—that deep place where the leader we hope to become lives—is eroding. Then up goes the pressure for even greater performance, and down goes our chance to become the person we know we can be. It's an inner management problem. We may have all the outer trappings of success, but unless we have the inner tools, our hopes, goals and ambitions start leaking away.

The leak can become a flow. We may cross the vital line of being motivated by and joyful about our circumstances. We can even head past a state of victimhood toward a state of desperate numbness. Job and career setbacks are always the outcome.

> The pressure of job performance erodes the balance at our inner core. Without using inner management tools, negative consequences are inevitable.

No wonder we use words like "pain."

How do I know? I'm speaking from my own experience. At one point, my inner core was so eroded that I got myself fired as CEO of a global business.

There I was traveling the world, being the big boss, great salary, and always jet-lagged. But inwardly, at my core, I was adrift and in pain. I made huge mistakes of judgment—ethical and commercial—and got my just desserts.

One moment I was competitive, hungry and driven. The next, I was being frog-marched out of my office. The memory of arriving home to my wife and baby mid-morning with no job, no car and an empty briefcase makes me cringe to this day.

That was quite a few years ago. Since then, I've met thousands of business leaders and asked how they feel at their inner core.

In today's fast-paced world, they say, the normal ups and downs of leading become far more peppered with deeper concerns, like the fear of management changes, worries about career and job security, even troubles with abusive colleagues. These things, they say, dull their hearts, sap their energies, and often leave this unspoken feeling of one's career veering off-course.

"I always wanted my leadership to make a truly meaningful impact in people's lives, including my own," admitted Brenda, the President of a medium sized U.S. company. "I've lost my way. That vision's gone. There's constant pressure and no time to think about whether I'm helping my own journey, let alone other people. I've become all action and very little meaning."

Please don't think I'm some kind of doom merchant. I've also enjoyed lots of stories of great achievements, incredible teamwork, and huge bonus payouts. But these days, thanks largely to the incredible pace of change, I see an emerging epidemic of people struggling to find joy in a life completely out of balance. One way or another, it touches us all.

And it's not just at work. This Senior Manager, Jack, is typical.

"You and my wife can tell me a thousand times that I'm working too many hours, but how can I stop? Even on vacations I'm constantly responding to emails. Just because I'm not there doesn't mean the business decisions stop happening. I dread to think of the consequences if I don't stay in constant contact. My family just has to put up with it."

This isn't leadership theory. It's the leadership reality of today for us all.

My question is: Does it have to be this way?

Does wanting to lead people and make a meaningful impact in life mean letting our joyful essence be drained or sucked right out? Does the price of determination and career aspiration have to be missing rest, losing connection with our families, and missing the satisfaction behind our deeper purpose for having a career in the first place?

I say no.

And I'll prove it to you.

My Core Has a Voice

After I was fired, I was deeply anxious about my future. I was full of shame, remorse, and self-criticism. Plus, I desperately needed to get some income flowing.

I was lucky to find part-time work at a company one hundred miles down the Pennsylvania Turnpike from my home. One day, driving back along the Turnpike worrying about my future, I heard a radio commentator.

"The key to being a successful leader is to know one's true purpose in life."

I slammed my fist on the horn and yelled back.

"SO WHAT THE HELL IS MY PURPOSE IN LIFE THEN?"

At that moment, from somewhere deep in my mind, came a calm, still voice that replied.

Don't you think it would be good to do something for other people once in a while?

I pulled over and turned off the engine. A mixture of joy, relief, and mental clarity completely overwhelmed me. It felt like the machine driving me for many years had slowed to idle at last.

Somehow, despite being anxious, ashamed and largely unaware of my inner core, it had calmly sent me a loud message. There is a new pathway ahead, it said. Becoming a better leader and moving forward in my life was about helping others.

The feeling of certainty was huge. At my deepest gut level, I simply knew it to be true.

I call it my Career Turning Point.

For years I had focused on climbing the corporate ladder. The happiest people, I imagined, rise fast, deliver great results, earn the big bucks and run huge organizations. I learned to keep my customers happy, but not myself.

Rarely did I look at the chaos I was causing inside and outside my work. I totally ignored the calm voice at my inner core, as well as my friends and family, telling me that these broken relationships, these business problems, these feelings of anxiety, were being caused by this inner fictitious self I had created and believed I must follow.

Judging by my conversations with leaders since then, many of us have these moments of anxiety-then-clarity that turn us to a new and far more certain path in life.

Thankfully, most people's are less dramatic than mine.

But for me, after that voice on the Turnpike, my CEO ambitions changed rapidly. I started to listen to my inner core.

Chapter 2

The Core of Other Leaders

The Habits of Great Business Leaders

I'm convinced that the spark of being a great leader lies in everybody. We are all inspired by so many examples around us.

Whether we're in a business, a farm, a school, a hospital, at home, or wherever, at some point we all ask ourselves: Will I make an impact in my life by being a great leader, too?

What follows can be a life-changing decision to start looking beyond our own needs toward contributing more broadly to the world. This is where our inner core as a leader starts taking shape.

Usually, we start by emulating those we respect. I call these people my Personal Board of Directors. They're the living and dead people deeply influencing me, right at my inner core, as I lead.

If you had asked me to list my Personal Board before that day on the Turnpike, my dad, brothers, former bosses, and people in popular management books would be there. It was their beliefs, values, and way of working that I was living off much more than my own. But that day on the Turnpike, the voice at my inner core had me thinking at my

> Great leadership starts with a connection to your inner core. You have to manage your inner core before you lead others.

deepest level. I was forced to think about firing some irrelevant members in order to reboot my professional life.

Then there was the question of how I was to start serving. The "other people" in my life were largely business leaders like me. But with so many other business experts around, why would they listen to me? Might they be interested in my story about my inner core?

I wasn't sure. So, one morning I started calling each of them to see if we could discuss leadership and to see if sharing my experiences might help.

That's how my leadership coaching career started. I began visiting all kinds of leaders to discuss their views about the hot topics of the day. And once a conversation started, I quickly moved to questions that dug into the deeper feelings and beliefs at their inner cores. Things like the joy of achievement, loss of confidence, the pressure to constantly perform and make a difference.

In fact, I was on a mission. I wanted to know—no, I absolutely had to know—if others ever felt like I had felt, and what they did about it. Secretly, as I listened to each person, I was thinking: Are you a worthy new member of the Personal Board at my own inner core?

"Leadership is about two things," I said with a smile. "First, there's leading the outer world of improving business performance and building productive relationships inside and outside the organization. Then, there's the inner world of how you deeply feel right at your inner core. It's transmitted in everything you say and do. It's impacting everything and everybody, in a positive or negative way, as you lead.

"You tell me, as a successful leader, managing the outer or the inner, which is harder?"

I've had fun asking this of hundreds of successful leaders. Not one ever said the outer.

Not one.

Inner and Outer Connection

Intuitively, I picked up a connection between how a leader manages this inner part and his or her success. Leaders who outwardly seemed to have an excellent command of business and relationships were always able to manage strong feelings really well. These were feelings just like I had, but, frankly, that I had managed poorly as a CEO.

Many of the people I met were constantly dealing with fear, agitation, and isolation, each in their unique way. I pictured an inner patch of emptiness that can take over at anyone's inner core if they don't take care. Like a festering sense of a lack of leadership and self-worth that erupts into negativity and confusion, spilling outward into the organization unless it's under control. This short conversation with Brian, a Senior Executive in finance, is a great example.

> Your inner core has a profound effect upon the inner core and behaviors of people around you.

"I've just had a traumatic feedback session with my CEO," he said. "After working night-and-day and weekends for the last nine months, and having been told I was on the CEO-successor track, now the politics have changed dramatically. I don't fit the board's view of the 'ideal' corporate leader profile. My boss says he's forced to score me low on our new performance evaluation system. My bonus and my career options just went out the window. I just told my team, and you can imagine how they all feel. They're going nuts. Are we supposed to be more or less motivated by all this crap?"

See how the negativity at the inner core of Brian, due to one conversation with his CEO, quickly infected his entire organization. Is that what he really needed? Couldn't he manage his inner core to get a better solution for everyone?

Here was the leader's pain flowing down and across the organization. I wanted to help. I wanted to reverse the flow, even turn it into a positive.

My head kept saying: You're an engineer not a philosopher, what are you doing trying to help them with all this frustration? But my inner core, that Turnpike place in me that deeply wanted a life that makes a difference, was calmly sending me a different message.

Welcome home, there's real work for you here.

Chapter 3

What Really Connects People

Discovering the Powerful Link

Listening to leaders talk about business situations and their feelings at their inner core, I started to analyze the connection between the two. I was amazed at its power.

A leader who displayed anger or lack of trust, for example, was leading an organization where people were defensive, unresponsive, and performing poorly. Someone who maintained inner calm under extreme stress was running an organization that was well balanced and growing. People who could humbly admit their faults and ask for help were leading organizations filled with loyal, open and highly motivated individuals.

The more people I met, the more vividly clear this powerful pattern became. The inner core of the leader was reflected back in the outer world of the team or organization. I was seeing the organization, in some unfamiliar way, as a living manifestation of the hidden, inner core of the leader.

The pattern transcended the workplace, too. People who really understood how to manage their inner core were leading great teams in all areas of their lives. People, like I used to be, who resorted to madly working harder under stress, were causing chaos wherever they went. It was all too familiar.

My inner core spoke again.

Successful leadership is more about a leader's inner core than he or she realizes.

Again, the overwhelming feeling of joy and clarity. I simply knew it was true.

My own experience confirmed it. Plus, I could see it in successful and unsuccessful leaders in public life.

Luckily, this inner-outer connection was something I could get my oily engineer's hands on. I thought: What if, for me, serving others could mean helping someone manage his or her inner core? Wouldn't I be helping them create a better impact in the outer world of his or her organization? What if I could help them develop a better way of leading, especially when they are so stressed out? Could this idea be the catalyst that helps someone discover more of the meaning he or she really wants in this crazy world? And wouldn't I be learning a better way at the same time?

My spirit was on the rise.

At last, a practical way to follow the direction of my own inner core had emerged.

Try My Approach

Just in case you think I'm completely nuts with my inner core talking to me, let me point out two other things that came from my leadership conversations. First, leaders would invite me back to keep the discussion going and, second, they would pay me a fee.

I built a business out of it.

My business approach focuses not just on improving leadership performance. It embraces the powerful inner core idea, as well as the effect of managing the inner core on improving a business situation.

It's a bit of a departure from the norm. Some (how dare they!)

even call me quirky. No problem. I truly believe that the inner core of any leader is the most powerful tool he or she has got.

Sample my approach.

To start with, here's a conversation with a "regular," non-quirky coach.

Leader: "I've got this problem with my team. They're not performing as well as I want. They don't seem energized to achieve our goals. Can you help?"

Coach: "Let me talk with you and them quietly and confidentially. See how everyone feels. Let's use a thorough survey based on my high-performing team model. We'll have lots of data about the situation. From there we can think about changes you need to make. My high performance team model is very good. The whole thing will cost only ten thousand dollars to interview, survey and discuss the findings with you. Of course you'll also need my help with the change program afterward."

Leader: "Okay, find out what we're all feeling and get us performing better..."

Now, here's the same conversation with me.

Leader: "I've got this problem with my team. They're not performing as well as I want. They don't seem energized to achieve our goals. Can you help?"

Me: "What is it about <u>you</u>, especially your <u>deeper</u> thinking, that's causing them to do that?"

Client: "[Gulp.] What do you mean?"

Me: "What you see is your team reflecting back your own inner workings. Face that, figure out the inner adjustments <u>you've</u> got to make, and things will start improving immediately for everyone. No charge for telling you that truth."

It's a totally different starting point to a conversation about becoming more successful. The workings of the leader's inner core are as important as an analysis of the competitive situation and team. It's unusual in business. The subsequent conversations take place in a relationship where discussions about the power of the leader's inner core to impact performance are welcomed rather than being taboo.

It also often includes recommending people focus on managing their inner core and not on managing others. I often suggest they say or do nothing with other people. Given that I was kidding just now about not charging, it makes my business model quite interesting, don't you think? Paid to help them do nothing! Yet it can be so powerful.

> Your inner core is the most powerful management tool at your disposal. And it's <u>totally</u> under your management if you choose.

How valuable might it be for you to do nothing but get out of your own way sometimes?

John's Story

Here's a transcript of a coaching conversation based exclusively on the inner core. Specifically, it focuses on the idea, mentioned earlier, that I call Personal Board of Directors. It explains how other leaders—past and present—are constantly influencing a person's inner core.

John is the President of a service company. His team wrote to the Chairman complaining about his strong-arm tactics. He needed to respond quickly, and he sensed that something deeper within was part of the issue. I asked him to spend a weekend looking hard at the way his Personal Board was helping and hindering him.

We spoke on the Monday after.

"I spent the whole weekend writing and thinking about my Personal Board."

"Who did you find there?"

"I guess most men would say their dad is there, and mine is, too. One of the most honorable people I ever met. Also, Jack Welch who led GE years ago. I met him once and I'll never forget him. I love the things he says, writes, and does."

"Sounds good to me John, anyone else?"

"Unfortunately, there were

> Hiring and firing your Personal Board—the people that influence your inner core—can reboot your professional life.

two less than honorable people on my Board. One was the Chairman of the company where I had my first Division President job. He was six-foot-eight and three hundred and seventy-five pounds, and he was control personified. One day, he was so unhappy at a management meeting that he threw the pre-reading binder across the table at the Treasurer. Only just missed. I put him on my Board because I learned an enormous amount about business from him. Unfortunately, I adopted his angry behaviors in my own way.

"The second was a college professor I admired. He would create a moment of excruciating embarrassment for an individual who was not carrying his or her weight. It produced an intense emotional flash point in front of embarrassed people. I confess to doing it, too. It's so destructive to relationships.

"This weekend was an awakening for me. I've started to fire both of them and think I may have found a replacement…"

John turned the situation around completely by learning to manage his inner core much better. It started with reconstituting his Personal Board. He elected new members by recognizing the power of people he respects to constantly influence his inner core.

Chapter 4

Naming Your Inner Core

The Unique Core

Leaders in business get treated like trees. Old branches get lopped off, new limbs are expected to quickly sprout, and there's constant trimming to weather storms. The trouble is that the pace of change and all the superficial adjustment outstrip our ability to permanently change. The learning doesn't stick because of the constant barrage of pruning and sprouting. The deeper beliefs at our inner core become conflicted about what is or isn't right. We can even move toward a state of unfocused numbness. Career and job performance problems are the outcome, despite all the investment in learning.

There's a better approach. Nourishing the roots of the tree as we go. Especially the taproot at our inner core. That way, we grow strong limbs based on the power of who we really are. The result is more joy, more certainty, less confusion, and greater strength during storms.

Do you know why the usual techniques and popular management pundits of today are only minimally effective? There's a placebo effect. They make a difference initially because we believe they will work. This belief ignites our passion to learn and do better, but forgoes providing the actual nourishment to our inner core required for us to sustain our passion and consistently repeat our lessons learned. Our passion for improvement thus weakens in the stress of the real world. The lasting connection to our inner core was only temporary, after all.

Saying "there's no time to learn any more" is the symptom. How can that be true when we are all constantly learning? The truth is saying, "I don't know how to manage my inner core to get important things to stick."

No wonder so few careers are actually ignited by all the books, CDs and other motiva-

> Growing as a leader means discovering all the ways you can manage your unique inner core connection. Giving it a unique name is a great place to start.

tional resources, and no wonder people flit from one popular tool to the next. Trouble is, the more they hop, the more distant they become from believing in the power of their own inner core to help them.

To grow and feel more joy as a leader, we all need a way to build permanent, non-flitting connections to our inner cores. That's why I searched for ways to encourage leaders to get beyond the superficial and discover, or rather rediscover, the positive parts of their inner core. It's a deeper sense of who they really are and can be. By redirecting them to the oft-forgotten potential of their own inner core, and using practical concepts that connect at that deeper place, like Personal Board, I wanted to encourage a different, less flip-flopping, journey of growth. And, yes, it applied to me, too.

So, I showed them examples of how leaders in public life connected with their inner cores. I shared my own example. I drew pictures of the leader's inner core linked to the inner core of his or her team members. Then I showed them how people's comments, especially their team's comments, were a direct reflection.

"What do you call the inner core inside you?" I would ask as I sketched in one of my confidential discussions. "I think of mine as my deep sense of balance. When it's out of whack, all sorts of problems happen. When it's in-balance, leading seems less like cycling up hill, more like rolling down. What's your word for it?"

I was asking someone to focus on a powerful collection of beliefs, feelings and thoughts right at his or her center. It's unfamiliar to many business people and it can be hard to do. Fortunately, most people recognize its power to help or hinder them. And they certainly understand its impact on others if it is out of balance.

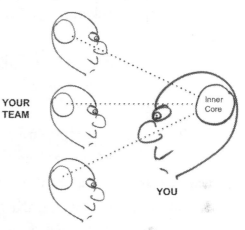

Terry's Inner Core

Here's how one CEO, Terry, describes his.

"For me, being a better leader requires deep insight into my strengths and weaknesses and how to really accept, understand and fine tune them. The place with these deep feelings about the growing leader I am is how I picture my inner core. It needs nourishment and refinement. When I have my core squared-away, I'm more open to seeing the truth of things going on around me. I attend to more of what people need rather than draining them. When I'm not squared-away I have moments of irritation, concern and agitation. Usually this means I need to do something different, like getting myself away from wherever I happen to be.

"Not that the environment itself is bad, but a change in environment is one way I preserve and strengthen my core. I've heard people say, 'Well, isn't that a bit selfish, making it all about you rather than the people you are with?' Well, if you don't take care of yourself, then you're not going to be able to help others properly. And that's a fact."

Terry shows why there's power in the name we each have for our inner core. It helps us in managing it for the good of people around us.

At one point I tried crafting a definition, but my Turnpike voice spoke:

It's the effect that's important. Whatever people name it, start there. Help them grow permanently by loving managing its power.

Again, the feeling of great joy and certainty.

I've discovered that being open to this simple idea is very important to my own inner core. It doesn't help me to preach my definition of my inner core as the ideal. But when I help them give their unique name to the idea it solidifies the basic idea that their inner core exists for them. It's my way of encouraging them to own the process of expanding and harnessing the power for themselves on their own terms.

But back then I needed a name for my own inner core. I wanted one that resonated deeply for me the way "squared-away" did for Terry.

I wanted a name that reminded me of its power to help me become a far better leader, a far better manager, and a far better person for everyone in my life, including my family.

I was saying "inner core" and "sense of balance" to business people, but I hankered after a name that really resonated deeply within me.

Making a Business Out of It

The more people I met, the more I loved the powerful conversations we had about the inner core, especially about how to sustain the desire to be on a leadership journey of great significance.

At last, my new purpose of helping others was finding expression through this idea of the inner core. It was joyful for me, and helpful for them.

Also, my business was starting to grow. It really helped that people seemed to like what I had to say and invited me back.

I created a simple model of successful leadership. I call it the Two Balls and a Bar Diagram.

The two balls at the top reflect that leadership is about creating a picture of the future—a more successful future—that inspires people to follow. Then, it's about keeping those people aligned and motivated to achieve it.

The bar at the bottom explains that a leader must manage their own inner attitude and behaviors to create the future picture of success and align

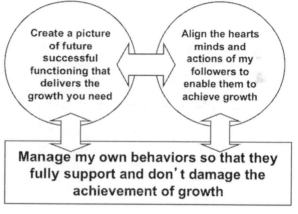

Create a picture of future successful functioning that delivers the growth you need

Align the hearts minds and actions of my followers to enable them to achieve growth

Manage my own behaviors so that they fully support and don't damage the achievement of growth

and motivate his or her followers.

Which is the most difficult part for you? Doing the work of the top two balls or the bottom bar?

There's no correct answer, but here's a hint. I never met a leader who really changed for the better who didn't say the bottom bar. Get my point?

It all worked great. The ideas were fresh, the clients were, for the most part, satisfied and the revenue flowed. They were learning the First Rule of Leadership, and they were enjoying it.

> First Rule of Leadership:
> To lead others to success you must first lead your inner core with excellence.

People agreed with the idea of connecting more with their inner core. But the tools to permanently expand the connection between the unique inner core and the outer world of business were hard to visualize and create. It was all so new for me. My mind was much better at the analysis and decision making parts of leadership. Plus, I still couldn't find a name for my own inner core that resonated in me.

Then I met a monk, and had two WHAM! moments. It sorted me out fast.

Chapter 5

Monkish Habits

Meeting Brother Daniel

A lapsed Anglican, I was sitting in the church at a Catholic Benedictine Monastery in the U.K. among monks dressed in their black robes. I was on a retreat with a friend, watching as the monks were praying and chanting. I was relaxed thinking how cool it was to meet and talk with these unique people. I truly admire The Rule of Benedict. It's like a sixth century business model.

Sitting there, my mind kept wandering. As so often happens, I was into the funny bits. I kept recalling the hilarious *Monty Python and the Holy Grail* scene with the monks in robes walking, chanting, and each bashing his head with a wooden board.

We were at a weekend event for business people. There was a lot of time to converse as well as a lot of quiet time for me to enjoy the funny bits. Whenever the monks went into the church, at least five times a day, we could all go and sit with them.

Seated with my eyes closed in the church, suddenly, out of nowhere, I saw a picture of myself in the future. I'm with my family. I'm dressed in a monk's habit. They are congratulating me on my decision. It was the most joyful feeling I had ever had. It was fantastic. It lasted for about thirty seconds.

I thought, what the hell is going on? My inner core sent me a video!

In a slight state of shock, I grabbed one of the monks, Brother Daniel, and told him.

"Relax," he said. "These things sometimes happen. It's okay. You're not going to become a monk. You've had a wonderful signal from within you. Just be patient. Maybe an answer is coming."

That's cryptic, I thought, sneakily looking for where in his robe he was hiding his head-bashing board. I started to relax.

"What do you do for a living?"

"I'm a leadership coach, Brother Daniel," I said, puffing out my chest slightly. "I help executives be better leaders in the United States and Europe."

"I see, but what do you actually do? What do you talk about when you get to meet all these important executives?"

"Well, I believe that what happens at the inner core is the most powerful part of a leader. By inner core, I mean the collection of beliefs, feelings and thoughts right at their hearts. How a leader manages this part is the biggest determinant of success in my work. When I meet with them we talk a lot about business topics, like sales results and team issues, but we also dig into the topic of this inner core. We talk about how what's happening in their outer world is a reflection of the inner."

"Oh, I get it," he said. "You help them take care of their spirit."

WHAM!

All my knowledge and experience suddenly jolted into focus. I could see that someone's inner spirit or spirituality and the inner core are the same somehow. The voice at my inner core was speaking to me loud and clear.

Yes! It's spiritual at the inner core. Ask him about a name.

Joy and absolute certainty engulfed me. I was back home again.

"Brother Daniel, you're very experienced in these things, is there a special name for this inner spiritual core in us?"

"There are lots of names. We all think of it in our own unique way. I think of it as God's infinite spirit that's inside me as well as outside. It's a very old question, you know."

"How old?"

"Moses asked the same thing. It's in Exodus, don't you remember?"

"Err...can't quite recall, I get very confused when it comes to infinite things. Can you refresh me?"

"Moses asks God: 'What name shall I use for you?' and gets the answer, 'Say I am the I am.' It's echoed many times in scripture. 'I AM' is who we truly are to be at what you call your inner core."

WHAM! Another joyful insight shook me. The inner core possesses all the powerful potential of who we will be before we become it. That's what I was seeing in my meetings: the inner core was being reflected in the outer world.

> Your inner core possesses all the powerful potential of who you will become before you become it. Managing it is thus managing your future.

I am your I am. I am who you truly are and can become.

"I get it, Brother Daniel!" I shrieked with joy. "There's this incredible spiritual power at my center that wants me to become all the good things I truly am. I'm going to call it my I-Am-ness. It's my spiritual core, wanting to come out and do great things in my future. I think I often fight it and get in its way rather than letting it lead me."

"We all struggle with that one. That's just part of living. I like that phrase 'my I-Am-ness.' It has an inner quality of being spiritually connected."

Spiritual Rather Than Religious

The retreat finished and I didn't know what to do. I knew at my inner core, at my I-Am-ness, that I had to follow it. But I was equally certain that if I visited a client and said I was his or her spiritual coach, they would most likely laugh or throw me out. Quirky, yes. Spiritually virtuous? Not me, mate!

Nevertheless, that joyful vision of myself in a monk's outfit kept coming back. What am I supposed to do, I kept asking myself? Should I get spirituality into my coaching? Isn't there a legal separation between religion and work to worry about?

I took a risk with a couple of people and tested out the idea that it was spiritual and happily (mis)quoted the passage from Exodus and Brother Daniel. Defenses came up. I said spiritual, they heard religious dogma. There's a huge difference.

In my thoughts and journal writing, I used I-Am-ness. It felt just great. But for others, I used inner core or spiritual core.

Some people are dogma-sensitive because of upbringing and life experiences. At my inner core, it's important to welcome the way every person chooses to name and manage his or her unique inner core. I want to help them be better leaders in the future. It's the downstream effect in their lives and the lives of others that's important.

So, I switched between spiritual core and inner core. I used little conversational probes to test comfort with the word spiritual in the workplace. No comfort? Stick with inner core and start with them naming it.

(If I may, for simplicity, I'm going to use the term spiritual core from hereon.)

Most important was that I pictured everyone with an amazing inner spiritual connection wanting to be joyfully revealed to the world in their future lives. Religion is one important way people tap-in, nurture and expand it, but I reasoned there are many possibilities. If the core is a unique spiritual place, I thought, aren't the nurturing and growing techniques also unique to each person?

And what about our working lives? Doesn't what we do in our jobs play as big a part in our spiritual growth as the rest of our lives? Isn't leadership work also spiritual growth work?

Writing about it in my journal and drawing pictures, I got myself very confused indeed. Eventually, I sat down and wrote a short paper[1]. I wanted to use business rather than religious language and see if I could clear my head.

My thinking was this: When you look at improving leadership in terms of expanding a leader's spiritual core, isn't the spiritual power already in the leader waiting to come out? Surely, I reasoned, it's also the same for all the people in the leader's organization, too.

Expanding the connection with the spiritual core at work can't be about adding something to a leader or organization. It must be about revealing and expanding the great stuff already there, in the leader, in the people and in the fabric of where they work together.

> Managing your inner spiritual core to be a better leader is about revealing amazing stuff that's already in you, not cramming more stuff in.

My idea was good, but I had been pruning and trimming trees, so to speak, not nourishing roots. Revealing not inserting. Blossoming not building.

When I finished writing, I printed out three copies of my paper and gave a copy to three people I trusted. The journey of those three copies has been incredible. You will see in later chapters.

---

1   Later published in The International Journal of Leadership in Public Services, Vol 6. Issue 2, June 2010 pp 68-72.

I was truly joyful. Here was a fresh way to help leaders think about improving their leadership. I was blessed with a cadre of clients who might be willing to try the idea. But how was I to get started without people being defensive or feeling I was being unnecessarily religious?

I had never come across a management tool that helped leaders reveal more of their unique spiritual core. I needed something that used words from business rather than religion.

Chapter 6

Market Testing

Sensing the Spiritual Core

(You can take the boy out of engineering, but you can't….)

Most people keep their thoughts about being spiritually connected in a completely different mental compartment from thoughts about work. Could I, using business language, help them link those compartments by revealing more of the power of their spiritual cores? And if I could, would it be possible to assess the impact where it really counts—in their jobs?

I was determined to test the benefits by expanding the spiritual core connection. But where was I to get the tools?

Practice what you preach, get them from me, said my I-Am-ness.

So I did. I opened my journal and tapped into my own creative power at my inner core. Then, with my Personal Board member Michael, an expert in consumer marketing, I decided to run a small consumer test on the whole idea.

> By sensing the state of your spiritual core and consciously improving it, you're making a better future for you and everyone around you.

First, I created a simple and practical tool to help a leader focus more on his or her spiritual core while working. It is a scale reflecting the state of one's inner spirit using business language. To the left is negative, to the right positive.

Before using this simple tool, I like to a) ask if you have thought of the name you use for your spiritual core, and b) suggest you take a few seconds to pause and get yourself into a more reflective mode. With these phrases, we are testing your deeper sense of the state of your spiritual core at your job. So, take a pause and get into your self-sensing mode.

I am not OK. Things are bad for me here	*I need to manage my situation better*	*I am feeling about OK with my situation*	*I am strong and feel growth in me and my team*	*I am certain I/ we have all we need to succeed*

As you read across, sense your spiritual core by testing your agreement with each statement. You should feel more of its power being tested as you move across. Somewhere between the left and right is where you land right now.

Calibration is what I call this process of sensing and positioning your spiritual core between the left and right.

The idea is that, whenever you calibrate, your spiritual core will naturally want to go more to the right than you are already. Try it. As you do, you will feel this internal wanting to get better. The implied benefit is that, if you accept the push and somehow move your spiritual core to the right, leading people will feel much easier and therefore be more effective.

For my market test, I printed the scale out on a 3x5 note card.

Also, I wanted each person to think about the things he or she can do that cause his or her spiritual core to move to the left or right. These are things that better connect or disconnect them from their spiritual core. So, to help with discussions, underneath the scale, I printed this double-headed arrow.

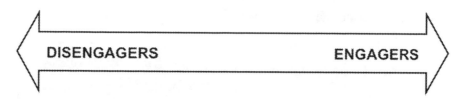

Activities that help a leader connect to more of the positive stuff at his or her spiritual core, and thus move him or her to the right, I called Engagers.

The opposite, things that move people to the left, I named Disengagers.

My premise: the more you do to keep your positive spiritual core engaged, the more to the right of the Calibration scale you move, and the better and more joyful your workplace experience and your future leadership performance will be.

Your Engagers and Disengagers are naturally unique to you and your situation. As an example, Engagers might be conversations with colleagues, achieving positive results or sharing difficult assignments. Disengagers are things like job security threats, unconstructive feedback or self-destructive thinking. (Much more on this later.)

Finally, for our market test I picked thirty leaders in separate organizations—half of them my clients, in both the U.S. and the U.K. To each one I gave a card, explained Calibration, and discussed the unique Engagers and Disengagers of his or her spiritual core.

"Please use the card during your workday," I asked each of them. "For example, every time you have a meeting, read the card from left to right, think about yourself and where you feel your spiritual core is at that moment.

"Also, try to do something, like one of your Engagers, that you know moves you to the right. I want to test if things improve for you. I'll survey your overall reaction in two weeks."

Dr. Stephen G. Payne

Spiritual Cores Being Revealed

"How has using the card helped you?" I asked in my email two weeks later.

For our consumer test, my teammate, Michael, had created questions. I'll summarize them as: "Tell me how it feels when you use the card and Engagers?"

> Engaging in behaviors that build your spiritual core connection opens pathways to a better workplace experience, more calm and much more joy.

and "is there any difference in the way people respond to you when you do?"

Twenty-six leaders replied. Michael independently analyzed the phrases in the responses.

To the question about how a person feels when they use the tool, seventy-two percent used phrases like "calm," "peaceful" or "relaxed." Here are some examples:

"I'm less stressed, more calm," said one.

"I feel more secure, peaceful and assured," wrote another.

"It feels more like I'm in sync in my life."

"I feel more comfortable with myself."

"I have a sense of security, and certainty."

I knew this feeling of calmness for myself, but was very surprised to hear the consistency among the group.

The voice of my I-Am-ness spoke again.

See! It's the spiritual core that is the source of leadership strength and calm.

I can't describe my joy when I thought about using that simple idea when coaching all the leaders I was meeting, especially those whose lives were so out of balance.

The result was even more surprising when Michael analyzed the survey answers about how other people were responding to those surveyed. A large majority said they were having great fun seeing such a positive difference. Here are some samples:

"I'm easier to be with! It's great."

"They seem to trust my leadership more."

"I see them also behaving in a more balanced, confident way, like me."

"I see my team feeling the difference in how I'm approaching them with a renewed energy and drive."

> People around you respond to your improved spiritual core connection by revealing more of their spiritual core qualities to you.

"They are more welcoming of my ideas."

The test worked. Leaders could manage their spiritual core in a business setting using business language and a practical tool. And the effects were looking incredibly positive. Here is Michael's summary:

"By using the spiritual core strengthening tools, the leader gains inner strength and a sense of purpose, and begins to view and trust oneself and others differently.

"As a result, others in the organization respond positively and become more open and trusting. The uplifting energy of the spiritual experience cycle begins. When the leader sees results in others and therefore feels an improved inner balance, the leader becomes more calm and confident and exhibits

> Seeing people respond joyfully to your improved spiritual core connection encourages you to connect to it even more. It's an uplifting, joyful spiral.

more thoughtful responses and deliberate actions. This behavior encourages the display of mutual respect, which in turn raises effectiveness, happiness and self-esteem. The experience cycle takes on an even more highly energized and uplifting upward spiral. It has a self-generating energy quality."

I rushed to show the results to my colleagues and friends on my Personal Board of Directors. They were so encouraging, especially Allison, a spiritually minded colleague.

"You're not just helping leaders find more joy with this tool," she said. "They're also discovering how to become much more balanced under the pressure of work. It's as though you are helping them discover a new equilibrium in life."

A New Equilibrium, said my I-Am-ness. *That's a great name for an organization!*

Moments of Reflection

Career Turning Points

Can you think of times when your life was hurtling down the wrong path? What messages were you receiving from your inner core? Did you listen to them? Did your direction change? Does it need to now?

Personal Board of Directors

Who are the leaders, living or dead, most influential in your life and the way you lead others? Are they all still relevant to the situation? Fire some if they are not! Who would you pick for a new cluster of mentors to help guide your career spiritually?

Naming Your Inner Core

How do you describe your inner core to yourself? Is it a name that acknowledges its power to help you become a great leader? Does it have a spiritual name?

Engagers and Disengagers

What are the things, like conversations with colleagues, achieving results or sharing difficult assignments, that you know for sure positively engage your inner core at work? Do more of them!

Big Leading Question

What's the relationship between your inner core and the inner core of the other people where you work? Think in terms of what unites you.

Part 2: Confident

Building A New Equilibrium

"We are the creative force of our life, and through our own decisions rather than our conditions, if we carefully learn to do certain things, we can accomplish those goals."
— Stephen R. Covey, *7 Habits of Highly Effective People*

"Growth is a natural process, and not an unnatural act of submission; it is not the pouring out of ourselves in weakness, but the gathering of ourselves together in increasing strength. There is no weakness in Spirit, it is all strength…"
— Judge Thomas Troward, *The Hidden Power*

Chapter 7

Moving "To The Right"

Calming the Mind

Because we each have a unique spiritual core, we also each have unique ways of managing our spiritual core for maximum joy and positive results. This means we have to take ownership of the journey of discovering what those ways are. Fortunately, there are many common ways of discovering them. Plus, the experience of listening and sharing joyful experiences with others can be profoundly helpful in getting new ideas to stick permanently.

Let me share a practical example of my own. Like many people, when I read across the boxes on the Calibration scale, I feel this desire to shift "to the right," to a more positive state of engagement with my spiritual core. By reflecting on how I feel about my

> Get more joy in your job by owning your journey of discovering unique ways to manage your spiritual core.

situation, and then reading across, my steadier and stronger state emerges. My bucking horse mind calms down considerably. I can let go with one hand and enjoy the ride. My faith in myself is stronger. I'm confident and ready for more. My self-critical mental chitchat calms down. Decisions seem more intuitive and less forced. I'm riding with purpose. I'm enjoying riding to win.

Caring for my spiritual core energizes me. I want to find more of my inner potential and move to a new and better equilibrium.

When I do this before I give a presentation or meet a client, it has a powerful effect. I get a more positive frame of mind, and I'm truly ready and listening. And because I feel more confident, I act in more confident and expansive ways. Clients respond similarly. Conversations become more productive. Things keep improving from there as the upward spiral takes effect.

One Senior Manager, Alicia, says this:

"My practices nourish my core. They shift my focus off myself and my own crazy thoughts. I move away from being a self-consumed, insecure leader. Moving myself over to the right, I find a place of joyful surrender and peace. I don't have to worry so much about what's going to happen next. I'm far more confident. Things always work out far better for us all."

In my case, in all candor, remembering to do it is often my greatest issue. When things push me negatively "to the left," I become increasingly uncomfortable. Fear starts to find traction in my mind. My negative mental chitchat starts. I become anxious and less confident. Doubtful thoughts emerge. My thinking and then my actions are weak.

That's the place I led from for many years before my Turnpike moment.

The Downward Spiral

No need to ask where we would rather not be. Over to the left, the experience of the life we crave and deserve eludes us. We are insecure and resentful, a victim of our circumstances rather than the master of our potential. Leading becomes a nightmare for both ourselves and our teams.

I said before that there's a modern-day epidemic of people with working lives completely out of balance. Why? Too much time being "to the left." The heavy demands of competition, money, and productivity push us there.

I've seen a pattern. Often we start a new job by loving the challenge, liking the pay and colleagues and wanting to succeed. Then, something happens.

Inevitably, the job is more complex and difficult than any training or previous experience can predict. Tensions build, as

> Engaging our positive inner core enables us to be the master of our own potential.

does the demand for better performance. We go over to the left if our spiritual core is not well prepared to help us.

Leaders I talk with, even Senior Executives, admit to strong, negative mental chitchat that spirals them down as they go through these times.

We all have this chitchat, things like:

"No matter how hard I try, it's not quite working."

"Will things ever improve or am I stuck here forever?"

"There's just no fun anymore with all this change going on."

"Will it be like this for the rest of my career?"

Let me get something clear. These are outdated, useless emotional programs—software viruses—intent on infecting our spiritual core. They can bubble up from the dark whenever we feel pressure.

Responding to them is what these viruses crave. The effect is to start the slide to the left and on down the negative spiral to victimhood. As we pay attention to our negative thinking our work performance gets worse. Then we tell ourselves that it's too hard to make a change, so we settle for less. If we push ourselves to work harder to try and improve things, we feel more pressure, more negative thoughts and more infection.

The pace of change around us doesn't slow either. So, the negative thoughts persist until we expect less out of life.

Miserable, gossiping colleagues accelerate the whole infection process enormously. Remember that the next time you complain to someone at work. You're sucking the joy potential right out of them.

> We all have self-critical mental chitchat that undermines our spiritual cores. You need tools to counter and reverse the negative spirals it produces.

Ultimately, the downward spiral leads to feeling completely out of control and lost.

"My job really sucks, my work-life balance is gone, my boss is awful, and the business is definitely failing. What's your magic formula for leadership?"

"Very simple," I reply. "I believe that what happens at the spiritual core of you is the most powerful part of being a leader. So, I ask you: What is it about the way you manage your spiritual core that helped get you into this awful situation? Are you willing to own your part? You won't get out of your miserable state until you do."

(Gulp.)

It's not just our mental viruses either. Life is full of forces that love to push us to the left. Mergers, takeovers, new bosses, difficult customers…the list is endless. Change can hurt us if we let it. Accepting that, and consciously deciding to use one's own tools, is what builds a life with far more meaning and joy.

And doing a little spiritual core work cures viruses fast.

Bill's Story

Take General Manager Bill in the U.K. on the fourth day of his new job.

"This place isn't what I expected, I guess I made a wrong decision," he complained.

"I don't think any of us can fully understand a job when we decide to join a company," I countered. "What's important is that you focus on the positive things you can achieve. Sinking and quitting is never the answer. I like to lift myself by saying an affirmation whenever I have these thoughts. Try it. I say to myself:

'I am strong…Therefore I can…Therefore I will.'

"It lifts me. Say it out loud of you can. It really helps reduce those feelings of regret."

Three weeks later…

"That affirmation really strengthened me as I got into my new job," said Bill. "Before I joined, they had set up a huge conference of global customers. It was three weeks into my job and I was the leader. Three days after joining, I could see a complete disaster coming, only fifteen people registered. My mind was telling me to get out fast. I used the affirmation repeatedly every day in the morning when I felt myself wavering. It made me so much stronger. We hit the phones, redesigned the program and had one hundred and fifty people fly in from throughout the world. The board members all complimented me on my leadership."

Bravo, Bill! From that affirmation, he's now expanded his toolkit to push back up the spiral and keep himself over to the right, where he is calm and confident. Affirmations and prayers are great tools for him.

Chapter 8

Staying "To The Right"

The Inside-Out Job

We all have patterns in our history that result from the negative chitchat viruses. The same failures, difficulties and temptations keep coming back because we don't attend to our deeper spiritual core. We become so driven by external stimuli that we can't muster the power to change from within.

Listen to this quote from Emma, a Vice President:

"Under pressure, I become my own worst critic. I have all these little voices in my head just waiting to tell me that I screwed up. I don't know where they come from, why they exist or the psychology behind it all, but I know enough that they're there and that they can suck me into some pretty destructive self-loathing that I pass on to my team."

Is she crazy? If so, then she's in a very large asylum called the modern workplace. Or is it simply her chitchat pulling her to believe and act on negative impulses? I know her. She is an incredibly gifted leader when she manages her spiritual core.

"If I hear a nasty remark about something I've worked on," she continues, "my first reaction is to get down about myself, think what a loser I am and blow it out of proportion. Sometimes, my internal critic starts nagging at me for no reason. So, I work hard at intentionally getting my inner spirit back into a positive space. The outcome is always better."

Do you want an experience of leading that is joyful and fulfilling, where interactions with colleagues are fair, and where you feel confident and balanced?

In a nutshell, do you want more of your life over to the right?

Learning to connect more with your spiritual core, especially when faced with obstacles, is a practical answer that really works.

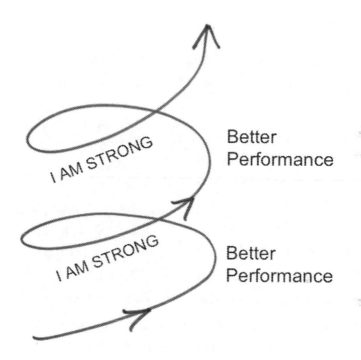

The pace of change is not going to slow down. For anyone who wants to sustain a balanced life in the future, we have to learn to adapt. At our spiritual core, we have the most powerful tools we can use to keep us on the upward spiral.

It takes a decision to accept our life experience more as an inside-out job. Our response to the downturns and problems then becomes less debilitating. We see them as valuable clues to learning more about expanding our spiritual core connection.

The market test proved it. By simply putting ourselves under its management, and then letting greater truths be revealed for us, our entire experience shifts to the right.

All my interviews with senior leaders, let alone the voice of my I-Am-ness, tell me that this is what it takes to build a far more successful and satisfying life in this crazy, connected world.

Spiritual Qualities

Yes, our job is about dealing with markets, customers, strategies and colleagues. But the way we feel as we deal with these things is determined by our deeper thinking.

If we learn to intentionally imbue ourselves with faith, balance, self-confidence, trust, creativity, determination, mutual-respect, caring, support and all the other positive qualities waiting to be revealed in our

> Accept your life experiences as being driven from your spiritual core rather than by the outer world. Your potential for more joy is now closer to becoming reality.

spiritual core, we are much more likely to go on to success, and much more likely to be joyfully satisfied with life.

We don't have to go down the spiral. Spiritual skills are like business skills. We learn the basics, and then adapt them to our unique personality and situation so we stay over to the right. Just as we learn to deliver new sales, cost reductions or new technologies, we learn how to reveal more of the amazing power at our spiritual core. The more we learn, the more we transform lives for the better, from the inside out.

Jim's Story

One Senior Vice President, Jim, put it this way.

"This spiritual core work all seems very counterintuitive and anti-productive to a Type-A person like me, but there is a really deep wisdom here. I've started the simple practice of reading and meditating in the mornings for fifteen minutes. My mind is normally filled with non-stop, incessant chatter at work, but this calms me and gets me grounded before the day starts. Somehow, I feel stronger at work. I'm no longer feeling that I'm helplessly flitting from meeting to meeting. I've learned to find that centered place in me more often throughout the day. I like this version of me much more. Judging from the nods and smiles, so does everyone else."

> Connecting to your spiritual core builds mental stickiness to your business strategies.

Like other skills, it takes time to intentionally integrate our unique spiritual core into our work life. Not everyone has the receptivity or aptitude, as I find out occasionally.

Driving home after a difficult client meeting where the ideas were completely rejected, I decided to complain loudly to my I-Am-ness about it all.

"It's just too hard," I insisted. "Not my domain, mate. You want me to help people make a unique spiritual core connection at their work, which happens to be full of zero-sum games constantly pulling them into defensive behaviors. You then want me to get them to reveal more of their spiritual core in solving problems, which it just so happens is shaped uniquely for everyone. Plus, I can't see this spiritual core thing, people can't describe it too clearly either, and the way it works seems subject to competing theological theories about infinity that baffle me totally."

Silence.

"There's more. I have to work with people at their jobs, not a nice friendly church or college. I'm stuck in there among all the interpersonal crap and competition, where the pace of change is

> At work, there's competition for praise and resources. At your spiritual core, there's an infinite supply. Where would you rather start?

frying so many people's minds. And, let me add, if I mention religion, I run the risk of being thrown out. Are we serious here?"

You're the engineer, answered my I-Am-ness, *develop some tools to help them.*

Again, the joyful feeling of absolute certainty.

With the help of my Personal Board members, that's what we did. We tried to be spiritual core-focused, but dogma-sensitive, by sticking to business language.

We started with tools that establish basic ideas from which anyone can develop their own unique approach for tapping into their spiritual core at work. Trying them out ourselves and sharing experiences became our standard.

Eventually we came to see these ideas and their ongoing development are part of an evolving approach to developing yourself and creating far more joyful experiences at work. We called it A New Equilibrium. It is also the name of the non-profit community we established for us all to learn, share experiences and support each other.

What's next in helping you stay over to the right by connecting more to your spiritual core? Well, you've already seen the power of Personal Board of Directors and a simple version of Calibration.

Let me share a few more of the concepts and ideas that work for me. Then you can decide to try some for yourself.

I did warn you that I'm quirky!

Chapter 9

The Power of Engagers

The Stevie-Wevie Bird

I was at The Waldorf Astoria in New York City, having been selected by The Conference Board to give the lunchtime speech during their prestigious leadership trends event.

I was to talk to two hundred top leaders about emerging leadership qualities for the coming years. Armed with really relevant research and some interesting material, I had rehearsed my presentation and was ready.

In the morning, I circulated a little at the conference. I tested the acoustics. All was fine as I waited in the dining room for lunchtime to approach.

Then, with ten minutes to go, I shot down the spiral into total panic.

I should explain that when I panic, I rush around in circles.

In my youth, my dad used to describe me as the Stevie-Wevie bird. This mythical creature madly flaps its wings while flying in circles that get smaller, smaller, smaller...until it ends up disappearing in a puff of smoke by flying up its own...well, you know where.

Not good for a leader to be watched doing this by team members. Up comes a major problem and there's me rushing around talking and thinking out loud. My dad used to stand back, chuckle, and wait for the inevitable puff of smoke.

There I was at The Waldorf running around in circles in the busy foyer. My material, I was telling myself, was awful. These famous leaders would expose me for the sham I really was.

So, I prayed the usual prayer of someone over to the left: Please, please, do a miracle and get me out of here right now. I'll do anything you ask!

My negative mental chitchat was working overtime.

"You're hopeless, you idiot. Why did you say you would do this? Clearly they are far better than you. You're going to look a fool. Look how confident they are compared to you."

On and on went the chitchat as I circled around doing nothing productive. I could see people starting to leave the conference and head for the dining room where I was supposed to be.

From somewhere the voice from my I-Am-ness sent me a message.

Practice what you preach: use an Engager.

Still in the foyer, I paused for a few seconds.

This isn't me, I thought. I need some help. Martyn, my lifelong friend and Personal Board member who lives in the U.K., came to my mind.

So, from The Waldorf foyer in New York I phoned him in England.

"In five minutes I have to give a speech on leadership to two hundred people in the Waldorf Astoria ballroom," I garbled. "They know far more than me about the subject. This is going to be a whopping disaster and my name is written all over it."

"Why's that, mate?"

"I've prepared this material—it's too thin. These guys are some of the most experienced leaders in the world. Now, they've got to hear this crap from me."

"Okay, let's take a couple of minutes. Be calm. Looking at the situation, just as a matter of interest," he said, "if you were one of them, what crap do you think <u>you</u> would like to hear?"

That made me pause.

"Good point," I replied. "They've been sitting on their bums listening to people all morning. They'd probably enjoy more talking and less listening over lunch."

"Probably," he said, being supportive. "But just chatting can be pot-luck in yielding anything memorable."

There was silence as we both thought about the situation. An idea came to my mind.

"You know," I shot back, "they've been listening to brilliant people all morning. I wonder what <u>they</u> think are the most important leadership qualities for the next few years."

"Great idea," he said. "Imagine if everyone leaving the

> Your most powerful team learning experiences involve great joy and sharing, initiated from your spiritual core.

lunch had some ideas they could actually use. It would be far better than any conference I ever attended. Good luck." He hung up.

The quick conversation restored me. I was back to the right. I was calm and confident.

Over the next few minutes I cut my material drastically. Instead of lecturing, I gave a few short points and then started a workshop over lunch to get their ideas.

Hungry people are a captive audience. I asked each table to talk together over lunch and come up with three outstanding insights for the future based on the morning session. I then invited people to share publicly over dessert.

We all learn some of the most important things in the strangest places. That day at The Waldorf, I learned something I've used scores of times since. Chances are there's a comedian at every table! When each table shared insights, they were not only fascinating, but delivered hilariously. We all laughed so much.

The applause at the end blew me away.

It's the power of learning by sharing and having some fun. Joy is always good. Use it.

Again, the feeling of certainty.

My Engager, the thing that shifts me to the right, had worked. Martyn had been my lifeline. When I let go of my chitchat and let his thoughts enter, a greater idea emerged. I just knew it would work.

The audience, by enjoying discussion and appreciating the content, pushed me further and further back up the spiral. My self-confidence was incredible. I was moved to the right. So were they.

I remember writing in my journal and saying thank you.

My spiritual core wrote back, in my own chicken-scratch.

You're welcome.

I thought, Wow! You write, too?

The Real Me

What would have happened if the Stevie-Wevie bird had spoken to those leaders? Polite munching while I gabbled on incoherently with far too much material? A puff of smoke over dessert as I disappeared up...you know where?

I recall myself rushing around the foyer of the Waldorf and cringe. Is that who I really was and wanted to be? What on earth do I believe as I go around in circles? Surely, not that I'm an effective leader.

Yet it's who I become if I let the stress of situations block the positive power of my spiritual core from supporting me. I surely want to spend less of my life leading people like that. It feels like the negative chitchat gets a tight grip on me. And what the world sees, especially my followers, is the outward effect.

It's the same process I observed in my conversations with other leaders. My inner spirit, in this case a very negative inner spirit at my core, was driving my actions and could can be seen by those around me. The flow from our spiritual centers to the outside world works in both a positive or negative direction.

> When you feel yourself drifting to the left, engage your spiritual core to rediscover self-confidence, deflect your negative chitchat and rapidly move you right.

The conversation with Martyn rapidly reversed my polarity.

How does it work that my spiritual core can do this? Does Martyn have some special power? Why did I call him and not my wife? Or other people I regard as positive Engagers?

No, he wasn't the person most likely to agree with me. Far from it.

To help you discover your Engagers, I'll explain my view of how it works. We need to go a little deeper.

Chapter 10

The Power of Belief

Beliefs Drive Action

What got me so motivated in that conversation with Martyn has to do with my beliefs. Let me explain.

I'm talking about positive and negative beliefs in my mind and how deeply I am attached to them, consciously or unconsciously.

We're all full of beliefs about how the world works for us and what things mean. Some are strongly positive, some strongly negative, and a whole bunch are in between. The best restaurant to eat at. The best schools to attend. The right way to tie a shoelace. The best soccer team in the world (Aston Villa).

Some of the beliefs are superficial and adapt quickly. Others, like Aston Villa being the best soccer team, go deeper (really deep, so don't argue) and become part of the fabric that we see as "the deep truth of my life." We have all got these deeper beliefs in our minds. They evolve slowly and govern the way we judge situations.

I use this ⊕ symbol (and the logo for A New Equilibrium) to represent my state of balance between all the positive and negative beliefs that exist in my mind. The ones I choose to attach to at any one moment, denoted by the position of the symbol, are motivating me to act.

So, digging deeper into the negatives, when I was the Stevie-Wevie bird at the Waldorf lunch, I attached to beliefs that said I am hopeless at doing my work.

These thoughts really do come up in my chitchat. I'm not sure where they come from. It doesn't really matter. What counts is whether I let them have their way.

But when I am over to the right, like when I came up the spiral during and after the Waldorf lunch, I believed positive things about myself, like that I'm strong enough to achieve any of my goals.

The Spiritual Uplift

The important thing is that belief drives action. If I look at the world and believe I'm unsafe, I may run. If I believe I'm hungry, I may eat. If I believe my job is no good, I may look for another. If I believe I'm about to fail, the Stevie-Wevie bird might come out of his lair. It is beliefs, from whatever source, that are driving me forward, especially those deep beliefs in my spiritual core.

The extent to which I attach to beliefs is called faith. It too lies in my spiritual core. As we saw at The Waldorf, it works in both a positive and negative direction. When I have faith that I'm no good and about to fail, I may freak out and disaster follows. When I have strong faith that I'm good, like attaching strongly to my belief that I can do well, I have a much better chance of succeeding.

Life's pressure seems to constantly push us in the direction of negative and useless beliefs. So, why isn't the faith I have in my spiritual core always strong enough to drive me?

My faith's like a bungee cord attached to the $\oplus$. When the cord is strong, I'm strongly attached to my positive beliefs about the world and me and good

> Beliefs drive action in a positive or negative direction. Your job is to know your beliefs and use your Engagers to build your faith in the ones that give you most joy and satisfaction.

action follows. When the cord is weak, my equilibrium is more over to the left. I run the risk of attaching to the corrosive beliefs about who I am or erroneous beliefs about my situation. It's how a virus weakens me. Unless I keep the bungee cord in my spiritual core strong, pressure and lack of attention weakens it.

(Note: Some people decide to attach their bungee cord to the $\ominus$ in their spiritual core. They enjoy strengthening their faith in destructive and harmful beliefs. These are broken people and I don't work with them. Neither should you. Look out for them. At a minimum avoid them.)

So, what does this have to do with my call to Martyn?

> Sustaining your faith in your positive beliefs when under pressure gives you an edge toward success and motivates the people you lead, too.

Engagers are integral to my positive faith management. I have learned to trust his ability to strengthen my bungee cord when I can't find the strength myself. Okay, I know that I should be more steadfast in my faith in my positive beliefs, but I'm a work in progress, too. We all are. He reconnects me to the positive pole in my spiritual core when I become disconnected.

It's the same process for all my Engagers. By Calibrating and discovering the things that move me and keep my spiritual core to the positive right, I have learned how to strengthen my bungee cord, my faith, as I do my job. Conversations with people on my Personal Board, for example, enable more of the positive beliefs at my spiritual core to find traction, rather than the negative. In turn, this leads to my actions doing much more good.

Did you know you're a bungee cord builder for people?

Here's a definition of being a leader to ponder: Helping yourself and others to enjoy staying attached to deep, positive beliefs at your spiritual cores as you work together in a chaotic world.

Chapter 11

Spiritual Practices in Action

Engaging Deeper Beliefs at Work

Yes, Martyn is one of my Spiritual Engagers. He boosts my faith when I trust him to help me reconnect to the positive beliefs in my spiritual core.

Be clear. This is not like an interesting, friendly and productive conversation with a colleague or boss about a workplace problem, not that those aren't helpful. This is quite different and all about bringing the power of my spiritual core to the situation.

It's a conversation where I made the conscious choice to place the control of my bungee cord, that is the faith impacting my inner balance, outside of myself in something I believe is greater than me. In this case, it was my faith in the power of the relationship with someone I trust. I let go of trying to control the situation entirely. I did so because I knew from experience that it would be restored in me ten times stronger.

"Here's my bungee cord," I implied as I gave my truth to Martyn. "Help me make it stronger, right now."

It's a faith building experience. It's a spiritual experience. It's a joyful experience.

First, I made the choice to put my trust in him.

This is my symbol for the greater power I put in any of my Spiritual Engagers when I use them.

Then I consciously let go of my own negative thinking that was trying to take control. As I spoke, I surrendered it all to him. I trusted that through him my spiritual core would be redirected to a far better place than I could manage alone.

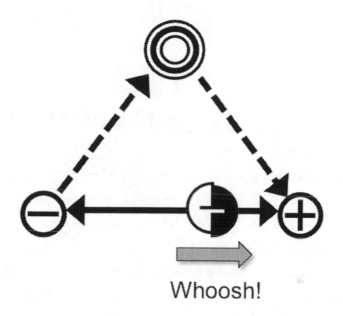

Whoosh!

I surrendered to Martyn (up arrow), rediscovered the true power of my inner core in the conversation, which then brought me quickly (Whoosh!) back to a more joyful place of belief in myself. And when I have that kind of faith, anything is possible. Even with two hundred business leaders in the audience.

As you consider your Spiritual Engagers, you should know that what identifies Martyn or anyone or anything else as my Spiritual Engager is this: By fully surrendering my negative state, I become stronger not weaker. The more I surrender, the stronger I become. Why? It's as though the amazing power of my spiritual core gets through when I consciously get out of the way of my own thinking. Believe me that power is far greater than anything my conscious mind can come up with.

This was not a momentary feeling of relief, but a shift to a deep feeling of complete certainty in a better direction. On his part, he was completely open, free of judgment, and willing to speak his truth, too. This is a spiritual practice involving someone who knows me, including my spiritual core, really well.

People argue there's no payoff from doing spiritual work in one's job. Or that it's all too mushy to learn these practices. I disagree completely. Look at this

> The more your Engagers help you release your negative thinking, the quicker the positive beliefs in your spiritual core will create new thinking based on your strength. Joy confirms it.

example of Martyn and The Waldorf. My increased faith and confidence was the subjective outcome. The brilliant idea about getting the audience to come up with the content was the objective result.

Also, I got a bunch of great business leads and a positive reputation with The Conference Board. All this from a five-minute conversation with a guy in England by phone. Isn't that incredibly powerful?

Everyone around us benefits when we use our Spiritual Engagers. That's because the power of the spiritual core working with our calm, confident mind can be simply amazing. And the joyful effect is contagious.

Terri's Story

Terri, a Senior Manager, discovered her best Spiritual Engager during a moment of stress with her team. She used a workplace surrender prayer. She said it a few times and got a Whoosh!

"This was quite a change," she said. "I started depressed by my whole work situation. I was sincerely thinking of walking away. Quietly repeating the prayer transformed me to a place of empower-ment where I could think and act more clearly—from my core—and no longer from a position where I felt I was stuck in the muck. Since then, I've been us-ing it first thing in the morning

> Working on managing your spiritual core delivers benefits not just in your job, but across your entire life.

and before challenging situations. I can feel my entire life starting to improve. I'm much more optimistic."

It's true. When you work on managing your spiritual core at work, the benefit is delivered across your entire life. But aren't we taught to compartmentalize our minds when it comes to spirituality and work? (Who teaches us that?)

"You can't leave behind who you truly are when you're in an organization any more than you can shut out the organization when you're alone," continued Terri. "Spiritual growth at work improves the entire collage of one's life. They're indistinguishable in how you think and how you behave. Those who think they can separate the two will always pay the price of filling their mind with unnecessary defensive strategies."

This fact that learning to connect to my spiritual core can impact my entire life inspires me tremendously.

I want all my activities to have more meaning, not just my coach-ing business. I want to feel that my journey counts. By revealing more of my spiritual core—my I-Am-ness—at work through my Spiritual Engagers, I build that certainty in practical ways every day. It's spiritual growth in life through work activities. They never mentioned that in the training manuals!

Below is another Calibration tool covering elements of one's entire life. It asks you to think about the words you use when you describe aspects of your life to other people.

Remember that when you say things about yourself the words work on your spiritual core just as much as that of the listener(s).

Just like the earlier example, you need to get yourself in a more self-sensing mode.

Read from left to right and sense your position by reflecting on the words you use to describe yourself to others. Be honest. Put an X where you believe you are right now.

WORDS I USE TO DESCRIBE MYSELF					
My Faith and Spirit	Lost Adrift	Occasional Temporary	Regular Steady	Improving Growing	Inspired, Energized
My Health and Body	Unfit Broken	Weak Limited	Improving Managed	Active Healthy	Dynamic Strong
My Mind and Emotions	Anxious Depressed	Slow Unhappy	Functioning Balanced	Vital Positive	Powerful Happy
My Family and Friends	Isolated Deserted	Distant Occasional	Available Helping	Supportive Important	Connected Thriving
My Home & Social Life	Adrift Unwelcome	Periodic Helpful	Together Happy	Engaging Rewarding	Exciting Enriched
My Finances & Career	Broke Bottoming	Too low Insufficient	Coping Performing	Successful Respected	Abundant Expanding
My Ideas and Creativity	Unwelcome Unshared	Searching Suggesting	Expressing Testing	Creating Learning	Powerful Inspiring

Would you like to move to the right across your whole life? Then start by working on the top row, your spiritual core. It drives your experience in all the other rows to the right.

Chapter 12

Intentionally Spiritual at Work

My Spiritual Engagers

A Spiritual Engager is something we do intentionally to reveal more of the good in our spiritual core into any situation. The feeling, and the test of a good Engager, is one of moving into a powerfully more calm, confident and joyful state as we do our job.

Don't forget that Spiritual Engagers evolve. Mine are unique to me, yours will be different.

That said, here are a few of mine that I am enjoying learning to practice as I work. Some I'm learning to do alone, others are more effective when I work with other people. The pattern I described using Martyn as the example—the surrender then do spiritual work to get a whoosh—is common to all of them.

On My Own:
- Silently surrendering all my worries in prayer and asking my I-Am-ness for a new direction.
- Stopping in the moment, and quietly affirming to myself that I am valuable, and have much strength to give wherever I am.
- Taking a break and doing a short meditation on a positive theme to clear the chitchat out. Soft music accelerates this for me.

<u>With Other People:</u>

- Surrendering situations and sharing truthfully with someone on my Personal Board.
- Giving my leadership experience to another leader who wants to become better at what he or she does.
- Meeting with a cluster of my Personal Board where we all share our progress in learning to stay connected to our spiritual cores.

Please don't think this is some kind of magic formula. It's not. Your Spiritual Engagers at work are unique to you and therefore different. So are your Spiritual Disengagers. When I use my Engagers during the day,

> Access your spiritual core at work by using your unique Spiritual Engagers. More joy and better leadership of others is the result.

I'm moved to the right and become joyful, certain and more confident. It's amazing how new ways of working emerge when I use them.

What about listening to me?

Whoops! Then there's listening to my I-Am-ness that speaks, sends videos and writes to me. It's truly become an amazing part of my life that keeps my bungee cord healthy and my pathway ahead clear.

I want to show you one method of connecting to my I-Am-ness I use all the time.

This is your quirkiness warning. It's a bit personal, but it's the only way I know.

Asking For All I Need

I was at a conference when I heard somebody describe the practice of writing a letter to your spiritual core and then writing a reply. I thought: How cool, I'll write to my I-Am-ness and see how it goes.

By luck, I met somebody who explained the process.

"It's like a normal letter, but it starts by addressing your spiritual power. In your case, you'll start: Dear I-Am-ness," she said. "Then you write whatever you have to say. Include all the things you want and don't hold back. Say thanks at the end and sign it like any other letter. Then take a short break and be calm for ten minutes or so.

"Then sit down, open a blank page, and start writing the reply. In your case, you'll start by writing 'Dear Stephen.' You just write whatever comes into your mind from your spiritual core until it ends. Try it, you'll see."

Back in my hotel room, I opened my journal to a new page and began.

"Dear I-Am-ness,

"I can't tell you how good it is to have this chance to write to you because there are a lot of problems in the world, especially my bit of it, that really need your help..."

Page after page of my concerns and needs followed. I included lots of requests to understand things, like how to explain leadership and spirituality, requests for support, and requests for new clients. Then there was my family and all the things we surely needed. I wasn't going to miss anything.

Just in case, as a bit of insurance, I added all the things I felt I had done wrong and apologized. Lots of requests. Would you do the same?

About an hour later, feeling completely purged of all possible angles of need, I signed it.

"Your mate,

Stephen."

Then I went for a walk for ten minutes and relaxed in the garden of the conference center. I felt refreshed. Writing about things always lightens burdens.

Returning to my room, I sat down, opened my journal to a clean page and wrote. The reply came immediately and calmly, much like that Turnpike moment. I wrote as fast as I could.

Dear Stephen,

Have you any idea how much I love you?

What are you worrying about all these things for?

The people you need are coming.

Write often.

Your mate,

I-Am-ness

Wow! I sat back overwhelmed. Again, the sense of certainty. The joyful feeling of calm and self-confidence was incredible. The need not to worry so much. The knowledge that other people will help me. I was so grateful.

Please don't think I'm "channeling" or something. It's not that at all. It's simply a way of connecting to my spiritual core as I go about my day. You will have your ways, I'm sure.

Since that first time, I've refined this discipline of writing to my spiritual core. It's a very explicit connection that reveals

> Communicate with your spiritual core and involve your spiritual core in your problem solving, especially the issue of finding your best Spiritual Engagers.

what I need. When I have difficult problems to solve, I often use it. It's become one of my intentionally spiritual practices in my job. I carry my journal around with me so I can I write on any topic anytime. Sometimes, I duck out of a meeting for ten minutes and sit and write.

It has never let me down. Not once.

Sometimes it becomes a rapidly written Q&A session; sometimes it's a long letter. Sometimes my I-Am-ness replies, sometimes not. (I take no reply as a signal to do nothing about an issue.)

It really helps me in engaging my spiritual core and reveal new pathways in my day-to-day moments.

I'll share a few of these letters with you later. You will see that, because I'm naturally such an outside-in thinker, I use it to get the spiritual inside-out perspective on any issue.

So, what are the best workplace spiritual practices for you to use every day? There are so many to pick from: reading, writing, sharing, praying, meditating...

In the community of A New Equilibrium, we help leaders discover their unique way of being more intentionally spiritual at work. We encourage each other to try things out. We are all on a journey of learning and sharing.

Let me encourage you to discover the best ones for you. Then you will feel the heighted sense of confidence and see the impact of that confidence in concrete results in your life. Each practice begins the incredible upward spiral of a life of greater meaning.

So far, we've covered general ways to access your spiritual core while you work. Now, here are stories of others to help you explore how to develop your spiritual core connection in ways that are unique to you.

Chapter 13

A Unique Spiritual Identity

Howard The Soul Fisherman

Howard is a manager whose spiritual core is ruled by self-doubt. His confusion in situations with any possibility of confrontation is palpable.

Alice, his wife, is the ambitious one. When a position of Corporate Vice President at her uncle's company came via her family, Howard got it, and they relocated.

In the first week of his new position, as he was settling in, he got a call from the Chairman's office asking him to stop by to see his uncle-in-law.

"Howard, welcome to the company," said Jack, who was just rushing off somewhere. "We're having a leadership team retreat this weekend at my favorite fishing lodge, and I want to make sure that you and Alice come. Can you? The group will be just over one hundred. It includes spouses, plus some of my industry friends and competitors and their spouses."

"Err...okay, Uncle Jack," said Howard.

"Best to call me Jack," said Jack, "See you Friday evening at the lodge. Got to go."

Howard hurried back to his office and called Alice to cancel the plans they'd made for the weekend. He'd been hoping for two days to work on moving in, but now, uneasy about interacting with his new colleagues, he started to worry about the weekend.

On Friday evening, Howard and Alice arrived late at the lodge. As they were checking in, they crossed paths with Jack and his friends going to the bar.

"I was hoping to see you a little earlier, Howard," he said. "I wonder if I could ask you to make the welcome speech tomorrow morning. It's a great chance for everyone to get to know who you are. Make sure you introduce Alice's aunt and me, and welcome the whole gang, the competitors, and of course the spouses. You know the sort of thing, I'm sure.

"Oh, also, as our new guy, we'd like you to give us your views on the company strategy and goals. What you think of our direction. What you find so great about us, and why you chose us. Inspire us all, Howard. I've been telling them all about you. You'll set a great tone for the event. But don't give the com-petitors too much, eh? We start at 8:30 a.m. See you in the morning."

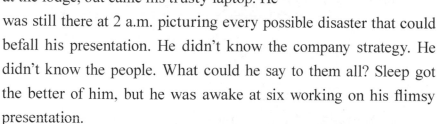

"Oh heck [or something similar]," said Howard to Alice, entrails liquefying, as Jack and his entourage walked back to the bar. "What the hell am I going to do?"

Kissing Alice goodnight in their room at the lodge, out came his trusty laptop. He was still there at 2 a.m. picturing every possible disaster that could befall his presentation. He didn't know the company strategy. He didn't know the people. What could he say to them all? Sleep got the better of him, but he was awake at six working on his flimsy presentation.

I can always get another job, he thought, as he cobbled together a few generic slides. By 8 a.m., he was dressed and heading to the hall with his laptop. When Jack's assistant told him there was no projector, his confusion kicked-in. He decided to escape. So, he walked out of the lodge to the lake and as he looked across, the terrible thought occurred to him that he was about to destroy his career in front of his wife and her family. Why not dive in and sink to the bottom away from this lot, he thought.

Just then, he noticed some fishing rods with lures leaning against a tree. Why not? He started casting idly, though he could barely concentrate on what he was doing.

You should hear the rest of this story as Howard told it to me.

"I was sunk. There I was, about to make an enormous fool of myself in front of Jack, Alice, most of her family, my colleagues and our competitors—pretty much everyone. At best, what I had to show was flimsy. I was in deep crap. I was trying to think of how to avoid embarrassing myself with the competitors so I could get a job with them.

"Then I just looked at myself standing there casting. Is this the person I want to be for this job? Is this what I've come to? I may have my doubts, I thought, but I'm a quick study, I love new technology, and I'm a great problem solver with my team. Why am I feeling so defeated?

"Immediately, two things happened. First, Alice called me to come up to the fishing lodge where they were assembling. And secondly, I got a bite. I had an enormous salmon on my line that was thrashing about in front of me. I couldn't cut the line, so I landed it. By then, Alice was yelling it was 8:30 and to come up to the lodge. Uncle Jack had joined her and was waiting.

"The fish was a monster—at least three feet long—the biggest I ever caught. I couldn't believe I'd done it. I landed the fish, picked it up with both hands and turned to look at Alice and Jack.

"It was in that moment I saw my situation—the job, my wife,

the fish, Jack, the audience waiting—and I just started to grin. You people may not know me, I thought, but you've sure as hell got me for a while.

"I kept the fish in my arms and walked up to the lodge, past Alice and Jack. I just kept on walking. I burst through the doors of the hall with the fish, and everybody turned and looked. I stood at the front for a second until there was quiet. Then I said, 'Good morning everyone, and welcome. I'm Howard your new VP of IT. I just caught my fish for the weekend—I hope yours will be twice as big.' They loved it.

"I felt ten feet tall. I didn't give my presentation.

"I said welcome to everyone, and told them that the fish stood for the truth about me and my team. 'We're quietly with you understanding the depths of your technology needs. We're agile and will go anywhere for you. We're not so big that my team won't be quick to swim over to help. We're always looking for food—helping you grow the business.'

"Then I wished them all a great weekend. I forgot to introduce Uncle Jack and the spouses; I never even mentioned the strategy. I got a great cheer as I walked off and gave the fish to one of the lodge people. It was a fantastic weekend for Alice and me. People just kept coming over and saying how great it was."

Unique Self-ness

What happened at that lake?

Despite all his doubt, Howard was forced to focus on the truth of who he really is to people. No room for spin or half-truths. He was reduced to his true identity; the very core of what makes him uniquely Howard to the world. No made-up images conforming to what others expect to hear, no politically correct language. Either the truth of who he really is was good enough, or it wasn't. Not his strengths or weaknesses, not his performance rating, not even his wife's opinion. It was his unique Howard-ness at his very core.

And when he stood, before the judges and jury of his life and career, showed it, and spoke it out loud, guess what? He shifted to the right.

Yes, Howard has many doubts, but at his spiritual core he has this modest determination, this gentle way of understanding

> Whenever you focus on the positive, unchanging qualities of the essence of your spiritual core, you revive the joyful, confident experience of knowing the truth of who you can become.

things, and an incredible ability to be flexible so problems get solved quickly. There's constancy to these things about him. He carries it wherever he goes in life. Just ask Alice.

When he stood and told the truth of who he is at his core, symbolized by the Fish, he found his spiritual core connection. Up the spiral he came to that confident leadership place. People saw it and responded with their support.

Do you know your Fish? I mean your unique positive qualities— or unique self-ness—that you bring to work and indeed everywhere you go? Do you hold it out in front of you, say it to people, and feel the shift to the right?

Do you get their support, despite missing things they need?

This is not the same as your job skills or strengths. Not your CV summary or your career goals. It's the distillation of all the good things about you into a unique Spiritual Identity that you take with you through your life, especially at work. It's the gift of you to the world that you can deeply believe in. When you affirm these positive things about you, or people point them out, you just simply know at your core that it is who you are and who you always will be.

It's the beautiful unchanging natural good of your spiritual core that you take with you into every meeting, every presentation, every interview—in fact, wherever you go in life. Reminding yourself of it is powerful. By recognizing the unique good at your spiritual core, you release some of it into the situation in front of you.

My unique Stephen-ness, my Fish, my Spiritual Identity:

Imaginative,

Quick, playful and teasing,

Bold and strong when confident,

Serves and helps people,

Mentally models everything.

There is a knowing in writing them, a sense of constancy and a sense of true purpose about my whole life experience.

The pressures of society and job push each of us into trying to be somebody we are not. We feel we must conform to somebody else's model of "great." We so want to please others that we let go of our identity and try to become like them. Too much of this, and down the spiral we go.

> Joy at work is good. Analyze the things that bring you deep joy at work. In those moments, your Spiritual Identity is showing itself to others.

But when we say or write our Spiritual Identity we are brought back to the right. We feel an affirming…

This is who I AM and I love it.

And that's always when we do our best work.

"When I realized that I wanted my life to have meaning," said Senior Director Katherine, "I knew I wanted to be engaged at the deepest levels of my capacity and desire. That meant finding the ways for my unique Spiritual Identity to find expression through my work. I try to remind myself every day who I truly am.

"Focusing on my uniqueness every day brings power to my words and the impact they have on others. It also helps me to delegate to others the things that don't 'fit' my identity. This is real leadership work that I thoroughly enjoy. I love the taste of it."

Knowing, writing, and saying your Fish is a spiritual practice. It's another way of surrendering all the chitchat and becoming assured of the bounties we have always had. Revealing not inserting. Inside-out, not outside-in. You are already strong enough.

What's your Fish?

I can give you some clues as to how to find it.

The sense of being fully, spiritually connected to your core at work is a joyful experience, so looking at the things you do in your life that give you joy is a huge clue. Try writing a list of the things that give you joy and talking it through with a member of your Board. They will see your unique Spiritual Identity as the cause behind the effect.

Ask the people with whom you work: What are the things that I do that always seem to help us?

Ask yourself: In what situations am I always successful?

In the streams of your answers your Fish boldly swims.

Chapter 14

Affirming While You Work

The Paper I Wrote: 1ˢᵗ Copy

Recall back in Chapter 4 I was repeatedly seeing an image of me dressed as a monk. I had spoken with Brother Daniel and had my double Wham! To clear my head, I wrote a paper about leadership and spirituality and printed out three copies that I gave to three Personal Board members I trust.

The first of those three is a story about a prayer. It was created with some wonderful people. Don't forget I'm not a theologian. It's not my area. Volumes have been written on the topic. I've seen many categories, like "affirmation," "meditation," and "spiritual treatment."

> Workplace personal prayers, affirmations and meditations are common, valuable tools for surrendering to the power of your spiritual core.

For any intentional spiritual practices, the name is far less important than actually using it as an Engager. Prayer, to me, is interrupting the flow of my mental chitchat, inviting my I-Am-ness to take over, and reinforcing my faith that a better pathway forward for all will be revealed. It's my personal bungee strengthening, lengthening and tightening practice. Whether it's a quick solo mental affirmation or a group activity, praying gets me in touch with the true purpose at my spiritual core.

I gave the copy of the paper to Terry, a long-standing member of my Personal Board, and a very successful businessman. He was then President of a large services company and an active member of his church.

"Take a look at this paper, Terry, tell me what you think."

"Okay," he said, scanning it rapidly, and placing it on top of his briefcase to study when he had time.

He took it from his office and threw it on the back seat of his car.

Later, he was having coffee with Lou, who was just starting a men's group, ManTalk, at Terry's church. They were to meet every Sunday morning for an hour.

ManTalk needed a speaker. Lou was stuck. Could Terry find someone?

"Hold on," said Terry. "I've got this paper on the back seat of my car by this guy. I haven't read it yet. You read it and see if it fits. Perhaps he's your speaker."

Within two weeks, the charming and persuasive Lou had signed me up for a three-week stint as the ManTalk speaker. "You're not from his church, you're not even a good Christian, what are you doing?" said my internal chitchat.

I grabbed my journal and wrote to my I-Am-ness: "What am I going to do with these guys? They're all important leaders in their community. I'm not a pastor or proper Christian speaker. Who am I to do this?"

My I-Am-ness wrote back.

What works for you will work for them. Tell them your story. Share your affirmation.

My colleague, Allison, and I had created an affirmation and a prayer. We said them together daily to help us stay over to the right. They were really simple and could be said quietly to oneself. I was learning to use them and they were keeping my chitchat to a minimum so I could stay calm, joyful and present for clients.

Following my I-Am-ness, I chose to go public and prototype the prayer with Lou's ManTalk group. I printed it on a little card to give to everyone and decided to ask them all to try it.

There's been quite a bit of tuning since, but this is the latest version:

Prayer for Leadership Moments

God:

My working life I now bring to you.

By your grace, help me to reveal more of your amazing love as I serve you though my leadership role.

Show me the pathways and relationships that better glorify you and serve the highest and greatest good of everyone in, and associated with, my organization.

I am grateful to be your leader.

Amen.

When I arrived that first Sunday morning, every meeting room was already taken. ManTalk was homeless. Terry was away teaching another class. I stood nervously, pocket stuffed with cards of my prototype prayer as Lou assembled the group inside the enormous sanctuary. Twenty-five guys scattered in clusters among the pews wondering about this person who wanted to talk about spirituality at work.

Like Howard and his Fish, I had no choice. My Spiritual Identity took over as I jumped up after Lou's gracious introduction.

"What's the true purpose of your leadership?" I boldly asked them all.

"Making more money for my owners?" came the first response.

"No," I challenged.

"Helping others do better?"

"No."

"Being a visionary?"

"No. We're in your church. Surely, the single purpose of your leadership work is to glorify God. Spiritual leaders try to make sure that all their activities are fully spiritually connected. It's like a plank that undergirds everything they do. Figuring out how to do that in every working moment is the true leadership challenge for people of faith. Let's share our stories and learn how to practice our true purpose in our jobs."

The clusters coalesced into a group. Lively discussion followed. I had fun sharing the stories of being fired and my Turnpike moment.

"This coming week, can we run a workplace experiment?" I asked. "I have this prototype prayer I say in my job. I've created a version for us. Could I ask you to say it, too, to yourself and someone else throughout the week?

"Say it to yourself before team meetings, after meetings, before interviews and so on. I don't think it's for saying publicly. I use it privately. Try it in your leadership moments over the next few weeks. Here's the card, pick a partner and write each other's cell phone number on the back."

Over the following two weeks we all met and shared our experiences of working and praying.

Prayer Really Works!

Did the prayer work? Oh, yes!

Here are some real-world experiences from ManTalk members

and other leaders throughout the world who have adopted the prayer for their own use. There are many versions. But it's not the version that matters—it's using it!

"We were doing an aggressive reduction in headcount," said Keith. "Difficult decisions had to be made. I have one man of thirty years service who is very bitter about his job going. Then he received news a week later that his wife had cancer. It's the prayer that has enabled me to take a long view and not be driven into

> The effect of praying while you work is that the power of your spiritual core can enter into problem solving. Joy and better solutions are the outcome.

immediate panic by seeing us as harming him and his wife. Our concern for him, our assurance that he was very much in our minds, and providing practical help like time-off has changed his position."

Joe said, "Using it in my daily life before meetings and things has been transformative and so helpful. I'm far more confident. It's so simple and easy. I carry it around in my organizer so it's readily accessible. I say it on the way to work on the train, and in key moments during the day when I'm pressured. It diverts my mind to thinking about other ways to get help."

"I was in a fierce and protracted battle about an appointment which I wanted to make in my team," said Cynthia. "Our local HR manager opposed me. Using the prayer relaxed my resistance. I accepted HR's position only to find that my HR colleague then relaxed hers and the appointment was made."

Dennis wrote: "I had to present to the board asking for support for a proposal, so I prayed the prayer before I started. The result was great dialog and an enhanced solution all enabled by me. Because I didn't push my outcome, the revealed path forward was far better."

"That prayer card is a terrific starting point for me because it helps me to have points every day where I can really think about and remind myself to surrender to the guidance of my spiritual core," wrote Brian.

It's all simply the power of prayer as a Spiritual Engager. Try it.

So, that's what happened to one copy of the paper I printed out. What about the other two? Incredible.

Moments of Reflection

Positive Beliefs

Recall times when you were confident and succeeding. How would you have described yourself to others? List these qualities, start each line with "I AM..." (e.g. I AM clear thinking). Keep this list and read it before meetings.

Chitchat Viruses

What are your common self-critical thoughts? Write a list of them and on each line start with "I AM NOT..." or "I CAN'T..." followed by the thought (e.g. I AM NOT a good presenter). Burn, bury or eat this list. It's useless.

Spiritual Engagers

These are powerful things we do to let go of a situation, calm our mental chitchat, connect to our spiritual core and build our faith in a better way forward. What are yours? Think of things you do alone as well as with others.

Spiritual Identity (Fish)

Your Spiritual Identity is the timeless, good and self-affirming statement of who you truly are. What situations bring you joy? When do you always succeed? Your Spiritual Identity is showing there. Write it down.

Prayer and Affirmation

Have you tried prayer at work? Many people believe it's just something religious people do in their place of worship only. Take my favorite affirmation for a test drive: There's good for me here and I ought to have it!

Part 3: Connected

Expanding A New Equilibrium

"The team with shared belief in itself is most often the winning team."

— Ken Singleton, Retired Baseball Star & Sports Commentator, *YES Network TV*

"Again, assuredly I tell you, that if two of you will agree on earth concerning anything that they will ask, it will be done for them by my Father who is in heaven. For where two or more are gathered, there I am in the midst of them."

— Jesus Christ, "Gospel of Matthew," 18, 19-20, *World English Bible*

Chapter 15

A Greater Purpose

The Paper I Wrote: 2nd Copy

The second copy of my spirituality and leadership paper led to another revealing journey. This time, it centered on my spiritual core and relationships. I gave it to a lawyer and former client, Ted. He said he was interested in the concepts.

He left me a voicemail a few days later. "I don't like it. It's definitely not for me. I've just given it to the pastor at my church. Good luck to you with this mumbo jumbo. [Click.]"

I was a bit offended. People at ManTalk who were using the prayer gave positive feedback. The other ideas like Spiritual Core, Calibration, and Spiritual Identity (Fish) worked well, even when I wove them into my leadership coaching.

One General Manager, John, even took time to write to me about how his relationships were improving.

"It's helping me see a common bond with people," he said. "My mentoring and coaching discussions with my team are going much better when I use my version of the tools. I used to be worried about confrontation. Now, the conversations are much more relaxed, yet direct and productive. Some of the team members have just told me they are much more comfortable, despite the horrendous pace we are expected to keep up."

So, why did John get it, but Ted didn't, despite saying he was interested? In spite of all the superficially supportive talk, he and I were never properly connected. I'd hit his "mumbo jumbo" nerve. He felt leaving me a voicemail was sufficient.

"How dare he? What's wrong with the paper?" I wrote in my journal. "These ideas are so universal and good, why wouldn't he agree with them? Where did I mess up in my writing?"

My I-Am-ness wrote back.

Every thing, every person, every organization has a Greater Purpose. They don't all align with yours, you know.

Again, the feeling of joy and certainty.

For sure, I knew I had a Greater Purpose in life. It was from my Turnpike moment. It was "to do something to help other people once in a while." What was Ted's, and why couldn't he agree?

I also knew that organizations published purpose statements. They set out the mission in an inspiring way. I had one for

> Your Greater Purpose is your unique way of serving mankind by bringing more goodness into the world.

my coaching business, which was "serving clients better and growing revenue," but was this purpose great enough? I didn't know.

The Ted experience was frustrating me. I continued writing in my journal and decided to do a Q&A with my I-Am-ness.

"What is this Greater Purpose thing?"

It is your spiritual purpose for living. It's about bringing more life-givingness and goodness into the world. Think of it as a unique spiritual strategy that includes your job.

"I get the word 'strategy.' How can I tell if my strategy is a Greater Purpose?"

You feel joyful and see the good results of being connected to your spiritual core as you go about your work. You're able to see and feel the effect of it reflecting back at you from other people. You're able to reach beyond your emotions to a deep sense of knowing, of wholeness, of sensing a life journey toward a Greater Purpose that has real meaning. When you think of it, you WANT to keep going on the pathway.

"Very good. So, Ted is out of alignment with me, right?"

People are free to choose purposes or strategies. There are many factors other than you. Ted's strategy does not connect to yours in Ted's mind. It's his choice. Deeper alignment of two people starts with a shared belief in a Greater Purpose and truth. You two have neither.

"So, Ted's got a Greater Purpose, he may not know it, and if he does know it, he clearly doesn't think it's anything to do with mine. I guess we each choose our purpose based on where we are in life. No wonder we can't get on sometimes. It's rooted in our deeper beliefs and bungee cords."

I paused to read what I had just written. I wasn't clear.

"I need an executive summary. Okay, my Greater Purpose is a strategy for life that positively affirms my sense of wholeness and meaning when I'm living it. It draws on my unique Spiritual Identity and creates more goodness in the world. I have a choice of strategy in every moment, and my faith in it has a lot to do with how well it goes.

"I think my Greater Purpose is: Helping leaders from all walks of life achieve far more success by being better connected to their spiritual cores."

Say it out loud to test it.

I did.

"There's this big sense of knowing it's my pathway. It's a deep, joyful feeling."

Dr. Stephen G. Payne

Just then my phone rang. It was Ted's Senior Pastor.

"I received this very interesting paper from one of my congregation, Ted," he said. "I like it. It is very practical thinking and needed in the high-pressure world. There's someone I think you should meet. His name is Raymond. He's an ex-financial industry executive who was

> Deep alignment of people toward your business goals requires faith in a shared belief in the Greater Purpose of you and your business.

ordained and is now running programs at the continuing education center at Princeton Theological Seminary. I think you two will get on like a house on fire."

He gave me Raymond's number and signed off. We never discussed Ted or the paper.

Then, I met with Raymond, a charming and articulate reverend and former financial industry executive.

Now this was an alignment of Greater Purposes!

"My job is to create and run learning programs for people who lead churches," he told me when we met. "But we are very interested in expanding our reach to all leaders in society. Can you help?"

Oh, yes!

"My Greater Purpose is to help leaders from all walks of life get more out of their spirituality," I said. "All I've done so far is talk to business leaders I coach and a men's group. There are some simple concepts and tools we've created for all faiths."

Raymond and I were instantly connected by our receptivity toward each other's Greater Purpose. Trust and truthful conversations followed immediately as we shared our experiences and hopes.

"What would you like to do now?" he asked after a while.

Go for it!

"Could we run an event on leadership and spirituality in the working lives of people? Would you be willing to accommodate business people at your center? I'm willing to help with the legwork."

"Accommodate you? It's a great idea! Let's create something together."

Two people connected by aligning their Greater Purposes.

This began the annual summit of leaders of A New Equilibrium. We invited business leaders to come together to learn more about making the spiritual core connection at work. With the wonderful support and participation of Raymond and The Seminary, and with the help of one of my talented clients, Jim, we crafted talks and workshops entitled "Leadership and Spirituality."

We are connected by a Greater Purpose: to be better at intentionally bringing our spirituality into our jobs to get more joy and better results out of our work.

Our alignment to this purpose produces incredibly valuable shared learning experiences stimulated by the insights of speakers.

Don's Story

The following is from a talk by Don, a serial CEO, on the topic of connecting with people at a spiritual level at work. He is describing himself at a time before he sold his company and joined what he calls "the spiritually corrosive world" of Private Equity Banking.

"One day I turned around and saw that the leader I had become was not the leader I wanted to be. I had lost my connection to my spiritual core completely.

"How did I come to this realization? I was soliciting comments from my Senior Management team about re-igniting employee commitment and performance.

"Two comments from colleagues had such a profound effect. The first: 'I'm tired of having to park my soul at the door before I go into the office.' Second: 'The Company beats me up forty to sixty hours per week and then expects me to repair myself on my own time so that I come back for more.'

"All the comments were similar. They were profound in their impact. I was completely out of alignment with my colleagues. As a leader, I was clearly failing. Was this business a place where the spiritual core finds expression?

"People want to have meaning and be aligned at the deepest levels of their desire and purpose. I wanted this for them and I wanted it for me. I had to admit that somehow I had lost the sense of Greater Purpose for my own work. Is it any wonder they were not aligned?

"I wasn't sure how to get it back. I was in a world of organizational and spiritual schizophrenia.

"Those in my personal life would not recognize the person I had become. I'm a musician by love and passion. I cry at opera music. I can't go and see an animal movie without having tissues next to me. Classical music moves me and my soul in ways I can't describe. But in the office, I was this individual who kept that entirely aside. I was a machine—efficient, productive, disciplinarian, demanding, setting patterns. Was I myself?

"I found my personal answer in developing a spirituality based on organizational soul crafting. It is a means for leaders to enhance the organization's performance by applying a sense of purpose, culture and identity one relationship at a time.

- <u>First</u> the leader's role includes nurturing a spiritual environment in himself as well as the organization. To me, that means showing employees how to become joyfully immersed in the present moment.

- <u>Second</u> is creating and encouraging organizational manifestations of this spirituality. Kindness, humor, courtesy, compassion...The inner core comes alive in the daily moments of meetings and customer interactions.
- <u>Third</u> is to establish processes by which alignment between the individual's spirituality and the organization's spirituality are managed. There are enormous conflicts that occur daily.

"We have to remind ourselves that we are put on earth to increase goodness and keep that as our byword when dealing with colleagues and customers day by day. This is really how we become deeply aligned with each other. Leadership's job is to ensure this sense of alignment of Greater Purpose throughout the entire organization.

"What we did was to set about creating an environment in which we could apply what we really believed. The business results improved dramatically. I think people will remember the transformation for the rest of their lives.

"Now, I'm practicing the ideas in Private Equity Banking. Every day I pray: I hope I change them more than they change me."

Chapter 16

Aligning Takes Balance

Share and Listen

As Don discovered, without a shared sense of Greater Purpose, misconnection is far more likely.

Tension is the result. The sense of meaning and wholeness is lost. Emotions like fear take over and flood the situation. Self-seeking behaviors follow self-seeking strategies. Given the ethical choice between right and wrong, people grab for themselves or their company, not for the achievement of their Greater Purpose for working or their organization's Greater Purpose for existing. This is a huge leadership issue in today's workplace.

Most often, this isn't an intentional thing. It happens naturally due to the absence of faith in a Greater Purpose.

Take Boris, a Russian orchestra conductor. He was asked to conduct a short series of concerts with an American orchestra. On the first morning of rehearsals, he stood before the orchestra, asked for silence, and spoke to his team for the first time. "Do not concern yourselves with me, my name or where I come from," he told them. "You may call me Maestro. In the last year, I have traveled constantly conducting the greatest orchestras in Russia. My commitment and energy are incredible. I have led some of the greatest concerts of all time. You will need to perform beyond excellence if you are going to match that performance.

"I, your Maestro, am committed to taking you there. In the next two days, you and I will work sixteen hours a day and I will lead you to perfection."

Just then a voice from the orchestra said, "Hey, whatever your name is. Screw you. I'm going for coffee."

Boris says he is passionate, forthright, energetic and creative. It's true. It's part of his amazing Spiritual Identity. He is a brilliant man with a passion that inspires. Yet, he's an awful leader of people in some situations. People in the orchestra that day found him to be a boasting, bombastic bully. Was that his intent?

When it comes to alignment with people, even if they have a strong sense of a shared Greater Purpose, we can't let our Spiritual Identity be so strong that it pushes people away.

> Reach your shared
> Greater Purpose
> by being receptive
> to the Spiritual
> Identity of others.

Boris was so emotionally hooked on his identity that he lost his sensitivity to the spiritual core of others. His communication was exclusively about him. His strength quickly became weakness.

This can happen to us all unless we recognize that other people have a spiritual core, too, and that spiritual core wants to be heard, revealed and respected.

The orchestra saw him as aggressive, even angry. They knew their Spiritual Identity both as individuals and as a group. When they felt they were not appreciated, defensive barriers rose. Before he could go any further, Boris now had to repair the damage he created.

What a waste of talent and effort. If only he had been more receptive to the Greater Purpose of others.

Caring Carla

This is Carla. She's the opposite of Boris. She was my plant manager when I did my training. Her team meetings were an absolute love fest.

"I want you all to know that I care for you so deeply. Don't be afraid to bring all your troubles to our meetings, because a great team knows how to care for each other no matter what. The team that wins takes care of each other."

She was our mother, but on steroids.

Before we could do any problem solving, we each had to talk about our problems, family as well as work situations, because she wanted to care for us. She was just as bad as Boris in being out of balance between the sending and receiving sides of her Spiritual Identity. She cared so much for our welfare that she omitted to care for our Greater Purposes individually and as an organization.

Don't get me wrong. At her spiritual core, Carla is truly a loving person. She deeply cares for people's lives. Put her in a leadership situation with colleagues, especially young graduate engineers, and they quickly choke on all the love. We never did any decision-making. We diverted her from real work by fabricating situations to test whether her love would go as far as giving us paid time off to goof around.

"Carla, my dad got his foot run over by a car, what can I do?"

"Carla, why can't we have a team meeting at the pub?"

"Carla, do you think the other departments like us?"

Carla and Boris are just two of many archetypically strong Spiritual Identities that can also be a leader's downfall.

Your Snaggy Bits

John, a Senior Executive in a large pharmaceutical company, described these as the powerful parts of us that snag on others as we pass by if we are not careful. Since that day, they have been known as the "Snaggy Bits" of leadership. We've all got them.

> Be aware of the spiritual core of other people. Your passion for your Spiritual Identity can push as well as pull.

They are people's negative perception of our powerful spiritual core when we fail to establish equilibrium between the sending and receiving.

See if you can spot yourself among all the caricatures on the next page. Each face and expression tells the story of a Spiritual Identity (phrase above) projected too far (phrase in italics below).

They are gender neutral, so, for example, the enthusiastic woman top right position could be you whether you are a man or woman. Ted, to whom I sent the second copy of the paper, is pretty much the one at the center.

Boundless drive and energy

Insensitive drive & hostile aggression

Empathy and ability to see others' view

Smothering and hurting performance

Enthusiasm and eagerness to deliver

Over-driving without dignity and respect

Political astuteness

Avoiding responsibility and blame

Wielding and holding power

Fortress mentality and hostile boundaries

Carefully assessing risks

Fear, avoidance and inactivity

Attention to detail and controls

Overtly critical and stifling initiative

Data and evidence driven

Rigid, dismissive and inflexible

Building congenial relationships

Putting niceness ahead of results

Chapter 17

Connecting by Being Fully Present

It's Not About "Me"

What Don's story and the Snaggy Bits point out is that when people come together, they are not simply interchanging ideas and feelings. They are also sharing their spiritual cores.

Colleagues overlook this time and time again. Broken relationships and tensions are the result.

It's not that we have to be liked by everyone or feel good about everybody, or even expect our Greater Purposes always to be well aligned. But we can be respectful of the spiritual core of others that, like our own, is trying to find expression by procuring a greater good.

We show respect for others by first connecting to the spiritual core in ourselves. By managing our own connection with sensitivity and receptivity, we become a model. From our calm, confident place we can intentionally recognize, respect, and be receptive to the power of the unique spiritual core of others. We keep our ego and emotions in check. Our Snaggy Bits are far less likely to come into play. There's more joy for all.

For example, how does it feel to you when you are leading a meeting or phone conference and sense (often from all the typing) that people are too busy to be fully present? Does it encourage or discourage you?

Adopting a spiritual posture that welcomes the other person's Greater Purpose does not cause stress in conversations, but releases joy. This is true whether the other person is conscious of his or her spiritual core or not.

"By preparing myself spiritually for a conversation with someone," said Tonya, "I find that I'm interested in his or her faith and optimism about the direction the company is going. I start my conversations sharing from that point and then move on to issues. I get much more buy-in."

What does she do? In a nutshell, she calms herself by connecting with her spiritual core to the extent that she can find connection with the spiritual core of the other person. It leads to far greater productivity in conversations.

> Leaders adopt a posture toward other people that respects that they have a spiritual core, too.

Bob, a leader in a healthcare business, says it this way. "I can't see the spiritual core in others and recognize its purpose unless I get myself into a state of being fully present so I can deeply listen to someone. The way I do that is to calm myself and first become fully present and listen to my own inner core."

Terry, who runs her own training business, uses this idea at the beginning of her classes.

"It's not sufficient for me to be centered and receptive to the group I'm training. I need them to do the same for each other so we get the best learning experience. Too often, executives come into my classes busily texting and emailing, and assuming they can be half-present throughout the day.

"When I start my classes, I ask everyone to put the phones and computers down. Then I ask for thirty seconds of silence in which I ask them all to reflect quietly on their willingness to be fully present for the learning experience of us all. I also ask them to check in with their sense of integrity at their spiritual core.

"After thirty seconds, I begin the class. The level of participation and connection is always so much better for the entire event."

I use Terry's technique and recommend it. Whenever I facilitate a client workshop I ask for fifteen seconds of quiet reflection before the team activity begins.

"During this pause," I say, "please would you ask yourself how willing you are to speak all the truth you need during the session." I like to quietly pray for them during that time. Then we start the workshop far more present for each other.

The Payoff

Don't get me wrong. This is <u>not</u> about ignoring or accepting inappropriate behaviors or low standards of quality in people. It is about <u>how</u> you go about working with people. When you value the connection to your own spiritual core, you respect the same in others. Your greater faith within becomes greater trust throughout. The level of cooperation and possibilities from even the briefest conversation can be amazing.

Every leader should make a gift to people: The freedom to be your true self.

Bob, the leader in healthcare just mentioned, wrote this: "I have had some interactions that could be considered substantially less than 'uplifting or up-building of people.' It dawned on me today that it is my job to see and know my spiritual core is present in me just as it is in them, and that I must have confidence in that independently of whatever message they are delivering. Wow! It is my job. I don't see that on my position description."

What he wrote next is very, very important to being a successful leader over the long haul.

He wrote: "What an added burden, but what a <u>great liberation</u> that far outweighs the burden."

Yes, there is a spiritual reward for doing the work of fully honoring the spiritual core of others. It is the feeling of joyful liberation in yourself. You are released from the hold of your own over-controlling mental chitchat. Yes,

> Respecting the spiritual core of others relieves you of the fear of losing control of everything.

released to unleash your own Spiritual Identity to become more productive.

You can test this idea out.

Think of the way you have responded to your different bosses over the years and you will see what I mean. Think of each boss you've had, then ask yourself if he or she respected the greater expression of your unique spiritual core in the job you were doing. At the same time, for each boss, ask whether you felt you were fully engaged and successful.

Question: Were you more successful with bosses that you felt respected your spiritual core? If you weren't, go back to the start of this book.

Think of people you work with now—above, below and alongside you, including customers or suppliers. For each person, plot them on the graph opposite with an X. First think in terms of your willingness to trust them (x-axis). Be specific. Do you consciously give them the freedom to be all they can be at their spiritual core? Then think in terms of the productivity of the relationship (y-axis).

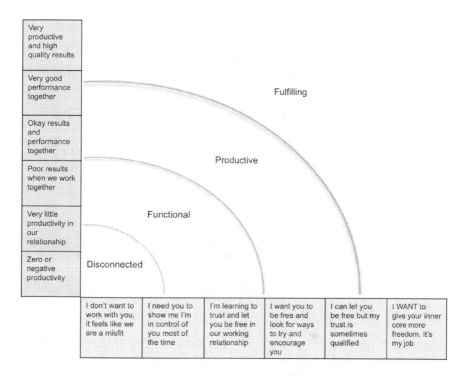

Very productive and high quality results						
Very good performance together			Fulfilling			
Okay results and performance together		Productive				
Poor results when we work together						
Very little productivity in our relationship	Functional					
Zero or negative productivity	Disconnected					
	I don't want to work with you, it feels like we are a misfit	I need you to show me I'm in control of you most of the time	I'm learning to trust and let you be free in our working relationship	I want you to be free and look for ways to try and encourage you	I can let you be free but my trust is sometimes qualified	I WANT to give your inner core more freedom, it's my job

Look at the balance in the quality of your connections. The more relationships you can have in the "Fulfilling" category, the better.

Would making the decision to fully honor the spiritual core in others improve some relationships for you? And improve your productivity?

It's your job!

Don't forget that there is a payoff. When someone senses you are fully present for him or her, he or she is more likely to be fully present for you. Communication then goes on the upward spiral, creating more joy and productivity between you.

The opposite? That's when I am not fully present for you or only present for myself. Then, in the extreme, you become defensive toward me because you sense I'm not connecting. You defend yourself and so I push and may attack. You defend, then I attack, and so on. It's the downward spiral of disrespect.

It's true that our spiritual core wants to become manifest as greater good in the world. But, as a leader, our spiritual core has to find expression by being well connected to the unique spiritual core of others as well.

That's why being fully spiritually present for people is real leadership work. Not just respecting someone for some reason, but honoring and appreciating deeply at your spiritual core that they have one, too, and that it is unique to them, their Spiritual Identity and their Greater Purpose.

And now to Liz, the recipient of the third copy of the paper.

Chapter 18

The Spiritual Team

The Paper I Wrote: 3rd Copy

Liz is a Senior Director in a U.K. healthcare company. I gave her the third copy of the paper. She's a passionate leader of sales teams with a reputation for delivering in tough circumstances.

She read the paper and called. "Great ideas, I'm going to use this to lift my entire organization at our sales meeting."

"Err...[gulp] it's okay with individuals, Liz, even in classroom situations, but in the setting of an entire sales organization? I'm not so sure."

"Look," she insisted, "the whole idea of being more centered and spiritually connected at our core is excellent. Life is so much more fun when I'm more calm and confident. It works on me individually. Why not the entire team?

"Look at my situation. I just inherited a team losing sales. They are unmotivated since a restructuring program was forced on them. Results have fallen, short-term fixes are everywhere. Morale is really bad. No trust, backbiting, and definitely no pulling together. These ideas about revealing the spiritual core could be fantastic for us. We need a fresh start."

I hear this problem from many leaders. The rapid pace of change leaves so many people feeling lost and adrift. Directional changes happen so quickly. Relationships never get settled. Team members become anxious. Emotion and personality start to rule rather than reason. Morale sinks to below the desperate numbness level. The incredibly creative power of being in a group starts destroying the group rather than growing the people and the business.

Is there a business team spiritual approach, I wondered? Can the individuals that comprise a team connect to a team's Greater Purpose and spiritual core and turn things around rapidly?

As I spoke with Liz, I decided to try it. But the Stevie-Wevie bird started to flap his wings. Caution! Don't go talking about the spiritual core of a team. If one dogma-sensitive person publicly takes a negative view

> The forces of change pull your team apart. The connection between your team's spiritual cores is the uniting force at your disposal.

by thinking it's about religion, the team chitchat could hurt them all, especially Liz.

Spiritual View of Teams

I took out my journal and decided to engage with my I-Am-ness:

"The Greater Purpose idea. How does it apply to teams? Liz's team members have lost their way. How do I help her to help them turn things around?"

Think of lots of circles representing unique spiritual cores of individuals and groups. Each core encompasses a unique Spiritual Identity and a unique Greater Purpose. They're all in motion, swirling and intersecting.

"I've got the picture of swirling circles."

Now, picture them in someone's mind. In the swirling circles are two special ones, one for the individual's Greater Purpose and one for the team's Greater Purpose.

The individual consciously chooses how the circles overlap and connect. In Liz's case, you call it aligning her goals with her team's goals.

"Okay, I see Liz's mind joyfully choosing to focus on how those circles overlap, which leads them all to succeed."

Now, see the similar picture in the minds of her team members.

"Okay, I see similar Greater Purpose circles in each team member's mind."

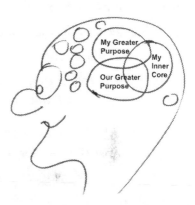

The productive work of the team accelerates when each team member chooses to overlap the two circles at their inner cores. That way the power of each person's spiritual core can be fully engaged in achieving the team and individual goals. Individual and group joy, clarity, growth and fantastic performance will be the result.

How can Liz help each team member find a new balance between the individual and team circles at their inner core?

"By sharing. I mean things like the team goals, customer needs and processes they need to improve."

In part, yes. She can get help, too.

"From her boss, Mario, the CEO?"

In part, yes, again, because Liz is a member of Mario's team.

"It's still a bit conceptual. How does she actually get people to get their spiritual cores engaged in this balancing act?"

First and foremost by always being receptive and connected to her own spiritual core. From there, she is receptive to that idea for them, too. The leader has a big say in the choosing going on in the

individual minds of the team members. This is especially true for the
Greater Purpose of the team.

"I saw that when I interviewed leaders. The attitude and behaviors
of the team are a reflection of the leader's spiritual core. So, starting
with Liz is right. Then if she could also get them each to understand
their spiritual core and Greater Purpose they will be much more
willing to choose to think about the Greater Purpose of the team. Her
faith helps them build their faith in the Greater Purpose, right?"

Right. And how can she build that faith in the team's Greater
Purpose? Don't forget that all circles can intersect and have Snaggy
Bits. That's why Liz talks about backbiting and not trusting each
other.

"They all work together on it?"

Yes. If Liz manages her
spiritual core well and shares
her Greater Purpose for her and
her team when they are together,
the team members can each
choose to follow suit and start

> Your team has a unique
> Greater Purpose and
> Spiritual Identity, which
> is far greater than the
> sum of each individual's.

connecting to his or her spiritual core, by aligning his or her Greater
Purpose and the team Greater Purpose. Team joy, trust, faith, clarity
and confidence will be the result.

"I need to summarize. The Greater Purpose of the team exists in the
spiritual core of a group. It has a unique Spiritual Identity all of its own
(in part a reflection of the leader's spiritual core) and a unique Greater
Purpose. By the leader getting each team member, including the leader,
to work on better managing his or her spiritual core, individually or
in a group setting, they will collectively be building the team Spiritual
Identity and revealing more of the team's Greater Purpose. The result
will be a better-connected and more productive team with more faith

in each other, plus trust and other nice stuff like joy, as they go about achieving their goals. This creates the upward team spiral."

Yes, faith in each other, faith in the purpose, faith in the creative power of the group.

"Just by each working on their own spiritual cores together? This is so much simpler and more powerful than the team building tools I've seen. I can't wait to test this out with Liz."

Steady! Spiritual and physical go hand in hand. There is always lots of real work to be done. Remember these three things:

1. *Freedom to Choose. Connection to his or her spiritual core by an individual is up to the individual, not the individual's leader. Encourage, model and persuade, but do not force.*
2. *Positive is Best. People can have faith in something that is negative or destructive, like not believing in the team, people or goals. There's no guarantee, but respect for each other is vital, as is encouragement.*
3. *Repetition Builds Endurance. People are bombarded by stimuli. It is natural for the receptivity and alignment to the team's Greater Purpose to be constantly pulled out of equilibrium.*

"Enough of all these swirling circles! We need a team Calibration tool. I'm off to help Liz."

Chapter 19

Team Calibration

Team Concepts

All the ideas about the spiritual core of individuals have their counterparts in a team setting.

Unique Spiritual Core — Unique Team Core

Spiritual Identity — Team Identity

Individual Calibration — Team Calibration

Individual Engagers — Team Engagers

And so on.

Whatever the complexity of the business situation, and surely it can be great, the mastery of leading others to be far more productive always stems from the spiritual core work of the leader.

I picture this expanded spiritual core of the leader traveling outwards to the team, through conversations and other kinds of communication, encouraging and building the spiritual core work of others in the team. This is where the overlapping of Greater Purposes happens. People have to be free to choose to connect their Greater Purpose to the team's, as represented by the leader.

Putting It Into Practice

To enable the spiritual core of the leader and others to be revealed, we took the simple Calibration tool you saw earlier and expanded into ten layers representing aspects of team experience. In each layer are phrases used in business situations. Calibrating by reading from left to right is just the same as shown earlier.

In a team "We" or "Our" can replace setting the word "I" or "My" in the boxes.

Read across and calibrate for you or your team.

For brevity, three of the ten layers are shown here:

Working here feels awful, but I have no choice, so I do it.	*My feelings go up and down, that's just how it is for me.*	*I seem to lose my confidence quickly in some situations.*	*I stay confident during difficult and stressful moments.*	*My role is all about keeping the whole team confident.*	*I am certain we are achieving all we need to achieve.*
No matter how hard I try, it is never good enough for people.	*Things just happen here and somehow I move forward.*	*I try to help situations by wanting the best solution for all.*	*In most situations, I find ways to get back on the right track.*	*I create solutions to make us better and take us further.*	*I know we find the very best solution in every situation.*
If I make a mistake I expect I'll get fired and be out of work.	*I feel stuck here without any chance of advancement.*	*I am willing to try to get to the next level of success.*	*I am ready for bigger and better job opportunities.*	*I am on a constant journey of learning and growing at work.*	*All my abilities are constantly growing just as I intend.*

DISENGAGERS   **ENGAGERS**

There are many ways to use this in a group setting. Individuals can calibrate themselves, others on the team, the team as a whole, or even individuals or groups not in the meeting or part of the team. The word spiritual is nowhere.

Calibrating is just the start. The real work is in the conversations about team Engagers and Disengagers, one-on-one and in group settings, that follow. This is precisely when people do the work of choosing to overlap their Greater Purpose circles. When they do, the subjective outcome is a deeply felt sense of shared purpose. The objective outcomes come from team decisions about Engagers and Disengagers that support the business.

Liz pioneered the idea with her team in the U.K. She emailed a few weeks later.

"The team of sales managers needed to learn to trust in their ability and to share thoughts and ideas without the threat of criticism and humiliation. Personally, I made every effort before the meeting to talk to as many of them as possible from the most experienced to the newcomers. Despite all the backbiting, I sensed an underlying passion for the business, its customers, and the users of our products.

"Then I used the Calibration tool with them in a group setting. I shared my own Calibration explicitly, including my own Engagers. Then I invited each of them to quietly calibrate for themselves.

"Then I asked them to repeat for their view of the team as a whole by replacing 'I' with 'We.' Then I opened up for discussions about Engagers and Disengagers and turned my attention to listening. The floodgates literally opened in front of me for two hours.

"A wonderfully positive team dynamic was the immediate result. Incredible when you consider the recent history. Some connections still proved to be difficult for people to make, because trust and encouragement was not the natural state of being.

"The blame culture was verbalized and stopped immediately. People openly brainstormed new ways to develop buy-in with each other. Openly providing feedback about how the team is working was agreed as our norm. You can feel the trust building internally and externally with customers. It's speeding up the business processes, too. It's all very creative.

"Doing this has also given me a huge feeling of personal growth, and provided the joy of seeing this team start to flourish and make good decisions. They have asked if we can come back to the tool regularly to develop trust and inclusion. Since then, many people demonstrated increased levels of motivation in their individual selling. You can see it in the results."

More Examples

Since Liz's pioneering work, many leaders have tried the tool and its derivatives. The power is in the fact that using it causes the spiritual cores of individuals to begin aligning individual Greater Purpose with the Greater Purpose of the team. It's the conversations that follow where powerful things happen between people.

Jim, a Senior Vice President in a manufacturing company, created an online version at his company. It is for leaders and their team members to calibrate anonymously. Each leader can then look at the aggregate results for his or her team and let conversations move on from there.

> Doing spiritual work as a team enables individuals to surrender their personal needs in favor of the team's Greater Purpose.

"Many functional leaders are using it," he reported. "We are using it in a very single minded theme: Building Trust. There's a lot of deeper stuff going on. It is helping us discover what trust means to the organization at the senior leadership level.

"We added a section for anonymous comments which really gets the alignment conversations moving in a positive direction. Each leader has a pulse on what is going on within his or her team. In every case, the tool provides a mechanism to open up dialog that is extremely valuable. Sometimes all it needs is for people to know the leader is listening. The tool is less of the focal point than the dialog generated. Just talking about the tool improves morale.

"Some leaders had never given any thought to what is going on in their teams. For some it's disheartening to see their team not quite as positively aligned as they would like to be. Eye-opening for others. The power is in showing someone that their own inner spirit can be lifted and in turn will lift others."

Bob runs a large organization, too. One day he invited his leadership team members into a conference room and copies of the team Calibration tool were ready for them at the table.

"First I asked my senior team to calibrate themselves. Then we took a break, and afterward I asked each person to fill it out for his or her team. I noticed that for those that were doing well, their score matched their teams. A few people had a huge disconnect with their teams. I just said 'that's kind of interesting!' and left them to begin the alignment conversations with their teams if they so decided.

"Two months later, I was surprised to hear that they were using the tool with their people to get them better connected. They were having a great result in getting and keeping people more engaged."

How does this work as a team building approach? Calibrating first encourages the individuals to suspend conscious individual and group beliefs, especially all the team negative chitchat. By doing this with each other, under the leader's guidance, a deeper level of surrender individually and as a group is created. The greater the surrender, the greater the amazing power of the spiritual cores in the conversations that follow. Alignment of individual and team Greater Purposes is the natural consequence. You see the joyful effect in every case.

It's very powerful. Leading a team is far more than setting goals and motivating people. It requires this kind of receptivity to the spiritual core of people, which always begins when the leader pays attention to his or her spiritual core.

But why stop there? What about connecting the spiritual cores of thousands of people in the largest organizations in the world?

Chapter 20

The Spiritual Corporation

Where to Start

What matters most when using these tools are the truthful conversations that follow. When an individual in a team starts by working on expanding his or her spiritual core in the presence of a colleague then the functioning of the group is improved immensely.

It's actually that simple.

You may argue that organizations need to have "the end in sight," hugely talented individuals, carefully crafted value statements, lots of money to invest or great communications. I wouldn't disagree about those things being important. But what comes first in any situation along the road?

If you wait for investors before performing, you will wait a long time. If you believe you need a picture perfect plan, you'll be so disappointed because conditions change rapidly. If you think you must assemble the most talented team, you will be constantly disappointed by the work of human nature.

Start with your spiritual core. Truthfully expanding your Spiritual Identity, reminding yourself of your Greater Purpose, respecting the spiritual core of those around you through team Spiritual Engagers, these are the ways to improve performance moment by moment. This is that upward spiral that builds amazing performance, exceptional

114

careers and a lot of fun and satisfaction. But does this simple idea work in a very large organization?

Picture yourself as the leader of the largest multinational organization. Using the metaphor from earlier, see the huge number of circles of Greater Purpose. All the different countries, languages, systems, customers, strategies and places people are working. All the products and services being developed and sold. All the investment and money flowing throughout the business.

Just think of the forces trying to pull the organization apart day by day. There's competition, regulation, global trends, people leaving and joining, money shortages, all constantly churning the organization. Can this enormous system have a Greater Purpose with a unique Spiritual Identity to which people can align? What about unique Spiritual Engagers? Let's not forget the pace of global change and the uncertain future either. Surely the global business can't be a reflection of the spiritual core of the CEO?

Hint: Is there something that has to be brought into the organization, or is there something there already that has to be revealed through the people?

Practical Examples

I was talking to Javed, a Senior Manager in Switzerland. He is part of a large U.S.-headquartered healthcare business, one of the largest in the world. He is a manager, in a department, in a country, in a global division. At lease four levels below the CEO.

"There's one thing all the managers I talk with agree that this company needs," he said.

"What's that?"

"A new CEO. Until he goes, we're never going to return to our glory. We're all just waiting for the board to realize it. He came to

Europe last month and was awful. He's personally taken a quarter of a billion dollars out of the company in five years. The company is going to the dogs with all the cost cutting he's done to fill his own pockets."

It's the spiritual core of the CEO expressing itself in the buzz, in this case very negative, within the entire organization. Not good.

> Large organizations are united by the alignment to the Greater Purpose of all employees. The CEO's alignment is the catalyst that is always on display.

A few hours later, I was talking to Amanda, a General Manager in a large U.S.-headquartered global food business. She's based in Australia. She went there as part of another global business that was purchased and absorbed into the bigger business rapidly. Acquisitions are notorious for demoralizing and stranding people in their careers. Like Javed, she is a leader a few levels down the organization.

"You can see that our CEO and her team have really good ideas about how we will grow," she said. "She believes that what connects people is a strongly felt sense of the organization's purpose. I agree with her. We all feel this at a personal and group level."

"How do you get that shared sense when you are so far away from each other?" I asked.

"We spend time talking about what the company's purpose means to us at a personal and team level. She has been very open in asking us to help her shape the long-term vision. I regularly reflect with my team on how we're all doing individually in living our purpose and how we can help her. My boss does it, too. It's got us all energized for the expansion project we are about to start."

What's the difference between Javed and Amanda? These large

organizations have many powerful tools at their disposal. Strategic planning, financial standards, compensation rules and corporate finance are just a few.

Both organizations also have a wonderful statement of their corporate values. They are published in documents and proudly hung on the walls. They're descriptions of why they serve customers, employees and owners.

The difference is in what Amanda calls the "felt sense of the organization's purpose." It's her CEO's belief in the power of a Greater Purpose. She, the CEO, places it first in importance for people. She sees it as a precious resource of the organization and knows its power moment by moment in helping people stay on the upward spiral and avoid the sense of dislocation and frustration that is all too common in a huge global system. It's not simply about written goals or values. It's caring about the Greater Purpose of the organization. It's about taking responsibility to help people find meaning in their lives, by expanding their spiritual core through their work.

Kevin's Story

Kevin is a CEO of a global business with a deep passion for the shared sense of a Greater Purpose of his organization. He knows that people want more meaning from their work and he knows that when each spiritual core is growing they get it.

"People want more joy," he says. "Retaining the brightest and best individuals in today's workplace needs something far better than systems and values. They need a strong sense of meaning in their lives. They need a CEO who is expanding his spiritual core so that they can do the same."

Kevin talks openly about the spirit of himself and his organization. He loves to find metaphors from movies—*Invictus, Secretariat,*

Money Ball—to keep the idea of "spirit" fresh in people's minds. He's been known to dress-up, dance, even jump on a stage and sing, in order to encourage others to share his commitment to having a personal, spiritual connection to the Greater Purpose of the company.

"Our Greater Purpose is bigger than any one person. It inspires a collective movement among the people in the company, starting with me.

"It is this: To provide the disruptive technologies that are going to eradicate cancer from the world. Every single person in the company is touched by this idea in their own unique way.

"It takes a shock effect to get people out of their comfort zone, to engage their unique thinking about the spirit of the organization. I want them to expand in all aspects of their lives. Then, they become more involved in their unique way, and more motivated and motivating of others around them.

> People around you are crying out for more joy and meaning from their work. Will your spiritual core be their catalyst?

"For me, when I'm talking about our Greater Purpose, it's like all my senses are working and I'm really getting all the meaning I can out of my life. I use these spiritual metaphors from movies to get to the heart of people and allow them to truly relate. People see parallels in their lives and understand.

"I find it most helpful if I can get people to resonate around a phrase and actually use that phrase in their daily work. It's like hitting the save button. It institutionalizes new ideas. It keeps the spirit alive long after meetings are finished. You'll see 'I'm all in' or 'Triple Crown' at the end of emails. It's part of the Spiritual Identity of the organization, and when you repeat it you are refreshing people at their core. I feel it in myself, too.

"Has it delivered results? We increased the value of the business from about thirty million dollars to six hundred and fifty million dollars four years later.

"There are always valleys where you go through some really tough times. The character of the organization is defined in those moments and if we each feel personally connected to our Spiritual Identity and Greater Purpose, it carries us through those times. It's very easy to get swallowed up by the short-term thinking of Wall Street and others that prevent you from really breaking through."

There's such a powerful energy to Kevin's organization. Their ability to personally connect to the Greater Purpose of the organization generates performance and loyalty like nothing I have ever seen. Bungee cords linking circles are everywhere.

Moments of Reflection

Greater Purpose

Look beyond your business goals. Look beyond your career aspirations. What is the true purpose of your work, your team, your company? Try writing them. The test is the sense of certainty you feel when saying them.

Snaggy Bits

When you project your talents with your ego unchecked the result is invariably damaged relationships. Can you think of times when you thought you got it right but those around you felt the opposite? What did you learn?

Being Fully Present

The leader who is fully present spiritually for people does the work of connecting to his or her spiritual core before conversations or meetings begin. What gets in the way of you doing this? Try not to be a victim.

Team Spirit

The team spirit improves when the leader aligns the Greater Purpose of the team with the Greater Purposes of the individuals. Can you remember such energizing team experiences in your life? Who was your leader?

Organizational Spirit

The Spiritual Identity of large organizations can be seen from the outside, too. How would you compare BMW with Fiat, Pfizer with Johnson & Johnson, Barclays with HSBC or Home Depot with Lowes?

Conclusion: A New Equilibrium

More joy, more meaning, more satisfaction from our work is the tip of the iceberg. Below the surface, for each of us, lies the amazing journey of expanding our spiritual core connection. No matter your pathway, this work brings value and importance to your role and to your entire organization.

See your Spiritual Identity as your personal, internal powerhouse of inspirational ideas and leadership potential. Realize that by engaging your Spiritual Identity at work and wherever you go, through Calibration and the power of positive Engagers, you will always find greater joy, calm and confidence.

Trust in the ability of your Personal Board to help you guide and right your ship in troubled times. Invest the energy in becoming receptive to the positive spiritual core in others, to understand their Spiritual Identity, and see the positive, productive outcomes you will create.

Never lose touch with your Greater Purpose and help define the Greater Purpose for your team or organization as its leader. That is the way to the greatest alignment and cooperation. It's your spiritual core that is the driving force behind the world you perceive. By connecting to it, the joy for you and others can be endless.

Welcome to your new state of being, your new equilibrium: calm, confident and connected.

A NEW EUILIBRIUM

A New Equilibrium (ANE) exists to energize and empower spiritually intentional leaders to fully engage their beliefs in the workplace.

Each ANE Leader is inspired in his career:

- Intentionally calling on his or her spirituality and faith in workplace situations
- Increasing effectiveness through greater balance, connectivity and sphere of influence
- Enjoying a unique lifelong workplace spiritual learning journey
- Participating in ANE's learning community
- Sharing spiritual experiences to enrich the journey of other ANE leaders

We share inspiration together in the ANE Community:

- Leaders and professionals — safely connecting, learning, applying, sharing, reflecting, influencing
- Supporting our learning through a wide variety of tools
- Encouraging, valuing, and sharing the impact of our experiences
- Being part of a spiritual, multi-faith, non-profit organization
- Supporting ourselves out of our genuine gratitude

www.anewequilibrium.org
@anewequilibrium